READER BONUS!

Dear Reader,

As a thank you for your support, Action Takers Publishing would like to offer you a special reader bonus. Learn how to become an Amazon bestselling author by downloading "How to Become an Amazon Bestseller—Top Strategies Revealed."

You have a story to tell. It's time to tell it.

If you've ever thought about sharing your story and becoming an author, this ebook will give you tips for after you've published. This comprehensive ebook is designed to provide you with the tools and knowledge you need to bring your book to life and turn it into a successful venture.

Ready to become a bestselling author? Download your copy today at https://www.actiontakerspublishing.com/bestsellertips. As an Action Taker, you know there's no time like the present.

BS Tips

READER BONUS!

THE
OTHER SIDE
OF
DIVORCE

Breakups That
Lead to Breakthroughs

Email: lynda@actiontakerspublishing.com

Website: www.actiontakerspublishing.com

ISBN # (paperback) 978-1-956665-73-4

ISBN # (Kindle) 978-1-956665-74-1

Published by Action Takers Publishing™

Table of Contents

Introduction

Welcome to "The Other Side Of Divorce: Breakups That Lead To Breakthroughs." This collaborative book includes the collective wisdom of women who have gone through divorce and used this difficult stage in life to make positive changes and life-altering transitions.

The idea for this book came from working with my divorce coaching clients. At some point in the process, everyone feels overwhelmed, and it can seem like the divorce will leave you shattered and broken forever. Finding the courage and strength to seize the opportunity to make positive changes is possible, and this book is a testimonial to the power and opportunity those changes create.

Change is hard at any time, but dealing with the upheaval of a divorce can make it seem particularly daunting. However, the changes brought about by the divorce can also create the space and time needed to consider what you want and what you need to improve your life in a deeply personal and satisfying way.

These stories, told by the women who lived them, are truly inspirational. They show how we can tap into our inner strength, knowledge, resilience, and passions to create an extraordinary life. While the stories are uplifting on their own, each author has also provided strategies, tips, and ideas for creating this type of change in your life.

Every woman's divorce story is uniquely her own. At the same time, we have shared experiences in having the ability to move forward and follow our dreams. As you read through these stories, you will find ways to relate to each author and the personal growth she experienced and continues to experience in her life. I encourage you to take advantage of the wisdom and insight the authors have provided, using the information in a way that integrates with your personal growth through the process.

This book highlights your ability to take a difficult point in life and use it as a springboard for something great. The results could be building stronger relationships with your children, friends, and family, finding your dream job, becoming an entrepreneur, embarking on travel adventures, or using your divorce experience to help others. The sky is the limit in the scope and range of changes you can make in yourself as a newly single woman.

The authors in this collaborative book have included gifts to help you with your journey. Take advantage of the tools and invitations offered to help you throughout your divorce and the rebuilding process that follows. You have unlimited potential to create the life you want to live, and we are all here cheering you on.

Be Your Success,

Mardi Winder-Adams

Positive Communication Systems, LLC

CHAPTER 1

Life Lessons Learned In Finding Out Who I Am

Mardi Winder-Adams

This chapter is dedicated to all the women going through divorce who have the courage, resilience, and self-confidence to know they are worthy of creating the life they want to live.

I didn't get married until my early 30s, and I thought I had done everything right to ensure a lasting, loving relationship. We both had good jobs, got along, and enjoyed many of the same things. We even discussed our future and had similar goals. However, I no longer felt we were a good fit after about four years together. The relationship wasn't bad; it just wasn't that deep, meaningful connection that I believed a marriage was meant to be. We were distant from each other and spending more time doing things independently. There was limited communication about things that really mattered, no discussion about our future, and we seemed to be drifting along in life without any specific direction.

At the time, I saw this as a failure on his part (100% on his part), and I was more than willing to overlook how I contributed to the distance and disconnect. A part of me wanted to make the marriage work, and I held on for almost a year, attempting to stick my head in the sand and pretend everything was fine. I didn't do anything to try to fix the problem; I just tried to stick it out to see if it would magically get better.

In all, it took 18 months to decide to file for divorce, which immediately plunged me into a whirlwind of decisions, adversity, and challenges that I did not expect. We didn't have children, but the conflict occurred anyway. It left me feeling guilty, angry, and frustrated. What should have been a simple transition in life became a dark cloud that seemed to be constantly over my head.

Even though my divorce occurred almost 25 years ago, it is still a vivid memory. I remember feeling overwhelmed by how a simple legal process was draining and all-consuming. I was always waiting for the other shoe to drop, and a whole closet full of shoes dropped throughout the process.

Thankfully, I had the support of my sister as well as that of some amazing friends. They helped me get through the legal issues and conflicts and supported me in many ways. I now know that divorce can be an incredibly isolating experience, and feeling alone during these challenges only adds to the stress. I am so thankful I had these people to count on during the divorce.

The Aftermath

In the first few months after the divorce, I was very content to continue to place all the blame for the breakup of the marriage on my ex-husband. I allowed myself to play the role of the innocent in the problems in the marriage, including the lack of communication and the lack of desire to identify the problem and attempt to correct the issues.

However, even at that time, there was this little niggling doubt about my contribution to the problems. Rather than dealing with it, I just wanted to get away and make a clean start, leading me to make some big changes shortly after the divorce. This included moving from Canada to the United States and marrying my second husband.

Moving countries is a complicated process, but it seemed like a choice I had to make. I felt very strongly that relocating and trying something new was critical to my personal growth. Looking back, I think this was the first step in making a positive transition in my life and giving me a clean slate to start making greater changes in myself, my relationship, and my career.

This decision propelled me into a series of career and life changes that, in retrospect, are genuinely amazing. Thanks to that one choice, I am doing what I love as a divorce coach, speaker, trainer, podcaster, and now also as an author. Each life lesson I learned and continue to practice has helped me to move forward with greater understanding, confidence, resilience, and self-awareness, and I'm excited to share them with you here.

Lesson One – Making a Choice to Change

Once I quit my job in Canada and moved to the States, I had to choose to change or continue in the same way. I knew I had to focus on myself. Not on the past, not on the pain, not on all the ways things could have been different—but on me. It wasn't easy at first. However, thanks to a forced hiatus as my green card documentation was processed, I had a lot of time to think, ponder, and make small and big decisions on how I wanted to experience life.

I discovered that many of my past actions and choices were based on what I thought I needed to do. You may have experienced these same ideas of what you should do in life. For me, it was to go to school and earn a degree, find a good job, get married, buy a house, and so on. While I had these things and enjoyed my career and life in general, they were not really what I wanted. This was a big shift in my thinking, leaving me feeling more than a little lost in what I wanted to do and how I wanted to show up in the world. I had an M.Ed and had been teaching for almost 15 years, and I had always assumed I would continue on that track.

But making that shift to focus on me, my needs, and my future was transformative during that forced downtime before I could start job hunting. It was hard work. It required me to look at parts of myself that I'd ignored or pretended didn't exist. It forced me to be honest about the patterns I had fallen into and how I had let fear and self-doubt guide my decisions. This included not speaking up for myself and simply following what I thought was the "right" path for success in my professional and personal life.

It also allowed me to examine the changes I wanted to make in my relationships. This included being proactive in communication and finding the time and space to have important conversations about our future, our desires and goals, and how we could support each other in achieving individual and shared goals.

I was developing an understanding of myself as a strong, capable, and resilient woman. As I let go of the blame and stopped obsessing over the what-ifs from the past relationship, I began to reconnect with that part of myself. Having a strong sense of self helped me transition from an employee to an entrepreneur and manage the day-to-day challenges in life, which wouldn't have been possible if I hadn't chosen to change.

Lesson Two – Building Resilience for Life's Uncertainties

One of the most powerful lessons I learned is how resilience helps me recognize my inner strength. After the divorce, I found that I constantly doubted myself. I questioned every decision and worried endlessly about what was next. I didn't feel strong, and there were days when I wasn't sure I could handle anything else going wrong or changing. But resilience isn't about pretending I'm okay or suppressing those feelings. It's about letting myself feel everything—the grief, the anger, the fear—while still trusting that I can get through it all and come out stronger on the other side.

Being resilient doesn't mean I don't feel pain or face setbacks. I do. But I've learned to respond to challenges in ways that honor my values and help me grow. My divorce has taught me so much about myself—like how to set boundaries, prioritize my well-being, and embrace a future I didn't originally plan for. These lessons weren't easy to learn, but they became the foundation of a more authentic and meaningful life. They became critical the day my second husband had a massive stroke and we were told he would never fully recover.

That resilience also helped me face everyday life at that time and today more confidently. The demands of work, family, and unexpected challenges don't stop just because I've been through a life-changing event. Some days it all feels like too much. But resilience gives me the tools to keep going, to find solutions, and to manage the stress when it feels overwhelming. It's not about having all the answers but believing I can handle whatever comes next and finding joy and gratitude in the many wonderful things I have in life.

I've also noticed how resilience spills over into every part of my life. The strength I've found through my divorce has made me better equipped to handle challenges and pursue my personal goals with more determination. And when it comes to relationships, resilience has helped me build healthier ones. By learning to trust myself and my ability to overcome hardship, I'm far less likely to settle for situations that don't serve me.

A big part of this journey has been learning self-compassion. I used to be so hard on myself, blaming myself for everything that went wrong in my life and believing I should have done things differently. But resilience has taught me to be kinder to myself. I've realized that no one gets through life without making mistakes, that it's normal and healthy to be imperfect, and that I deserve grace as much as anyone else. This self-compassion is a powerful tool for healing and rebuilding.

Resilience has also helped me redefine what success and happiness mean to me. Before my divorce, I had a clear picture of what my life was supposed to look like—a shared future with my partner, specific goals, and dreams we'd built together. When that picture fell apart, it was unnerving. But over time, I've come to see that happiness isn't tied to a single vision of the future. I can create it for myself, even if it looks completely different from what I once imagined.

I've also learned that resilience doesn't mean doing everything on my own. One of the hardest and most rewarding parts of this process has been learning how to ask for help. It may seem like a simple thing, but for someone who used to have a hard time asking for help, this is a huge win. Whether leaning on friends and family or seeking professional support, I've realized that resilience includes knowing when I need help and having the courage to ask for it. These connections remind me that I'm not alone and that shared experiences can bring comfort and perspective when I need them most.

One of the most empowering things about resilience is how it's changed how I see challenges. I won't say I welcome difficulties, but I've learned to see them as opportunities to grow. That doesn't mean the pain isn't real or that I try to put a positive spin on everything. It just means I've come to understand that every challenge has the potential to teach me something valuable about myself and my strengths.

For me, resilience isn't about being perfect or having it all figured out. It's about showing up for myself, even when life feels hard. It's about taking things one day at a time, finding small ways to move forward, and believing—especially on the toughest days—that I can create a meaningful, joyful life.

If you're going through a divorce, I want you to know that resilience isn't something you're born with or without. You can nurture and develop it, no matter how lost or broken you feel. It takes time, patience, and effort, but it's worth it. Resilience doesn't just help you heal from divorce; it prepares you to face whatever comes next with courage and confidence.

Above all, I've learned that resilience isn't about being unaffected by life's struggles. It's about allowing myself to be shaped by them in ways that help me grow. It's about trusting that I have the strength to rebuild, no matter how many times life asks me to start over. As I continue to build this strength, I've discovered that I have far more strength than I imagined, and it is only through challenges like my divorce that I exercised my resilience muscle.

Lesson Three – Changing My Perception

Divorce was a turning point in my career path, although it didn't happen immediately. I worked as a Domestic Violence Client Advocate and advocate for kids and families. I also completed my coaching certifications and became a divorce coach to help other women find the same strength and clarity within themselves. Looking back, I see how each step in my career path after the divorce led me closer to working with people going through divorce, which is my passion.

The emotional toll, the endless decisions, and the fear of the unknown can feel like you're drowning during a divorce. And yet, I also know that there are proven, effective ways to move through it. This includes ways to survive the process and come out on the other side stronger and more self-assured than you ever thought possible.

One of the hardest things about divorce is the way it seems to touch every part of your life at once. It's not just the relationship that ends. It's your routines, your plans, your sense of security. It's the little things, like who takes the dog to the vet, and the big things, like how to handle holidays. Every decision feels loaded, and the weight of it all can feel unbearable.

What I learned, though, is that you don't have to tackle it all at once. You don't have to have all the answers today. There's a kind of freedom in accepting that some things will remain uncertain for a while. That's hard for someone like me, who's always been a planner and a doer. But breathing became easier once I permitted myself to take things one step at a time. I could focus on the decisions right in front of me instead of worrying about everything all at once.

I also learned that it's okay to ask for help. For so long, I thought I had to do everything on my own. I thought asking for support was a sign of weakness or failure. But that couldn't be further from the truth. Whether leaning on friends, finding a therapist, or eventually working with a coach, I discovered that the people around me wanted to help. They wanted to see me succeed. And when I let them in, it made all the difference.

One of the most surprising things I discovered during my divorce was that I already had so many of the tools I needed to get through it.

At first, I didn't see it that way. I felt unprepared and unequipped to handle the challenges in front of me. But as I moved through the process, I started to recognize the strengths I'd been carrying all along. My ability to problem-solve, my resilience, my capacity for empathy and understanding—these were skills I'd developed over years of navigating life's ups and downs. They were there all along; I just had to learn how to apply them in this new context.

And I truly believe that you have those skills, too. You might not feel like it right now. You might feel like the ground has been ripped out from under you, like you're scrambling to make sense of it all. But I promise you, the strengths you need to get through this are already within you. They might be hiding under layers of doubt and fear, but they're there. And as you start to uncover them, you'll see just how capable you are.

Of course, none of this happens overnight. Healing takes time. Rebuilding your life takes time. And there will be moments when it feels like you're taking one step forward and two steps back. That's normal. It's part of the process. But each small step you take—each moment of courage, each act of self-care—brings you closer to the person you're becoming. And that person? She's incredible. She's someone who knows her worth, who trusts her instincts, and who isn't afraid to prioritize her own happiness.

Looking back, I can see that my divorce was a turning point. It was painful, but it was also an opportunity to rediscover myself. It allowed me to let go of the parts of my life that weren't serving me and to create something new in their place. It taught me that I'm stronger than I ever realized. It showed me that there's a way forward, even in times of dramatic change and uncertainty.

That's what I want for you, too. I want you to know that no matter how overwhelming this feels, you have what it takes to get through it.

You have the strength, the skills, and the emotional resources to face these challenges head-on. And you don't have to do it alone. Whether it's through the support of friends, family, or someone like me, help is out there. You just have to be willing to reach for it.

Divorce is hard. There's no way around that. But it doesn't have to define you. It doesn't have to be the end of your story. In fact, it can be the beginning of something truly transformative. It can be the moment when you stop living for everyone else and start living for yourself. The moment you stop worrying about what others think and start focusing on what you need. The moment when you stop questioning your worth and start believing in your ability to create a life that brings joy and abundance. These moments won't happen overnight, but they will happen if you focus on healing and moving forward with your life.

This isn't just something I believe—it's something I know. I've seen and experienced what's possible when you choose to focus on yourself, let go of the past, and trust in your resilience. And I know that you can do it, too.

Mardi Winder-Adams

Mardi Winder-Adams is a leading divorce coach for high-achieving women, dedicated to helping them take control of their separation and divorce. Her goal is to reduce the emotional and financial costs associated with the process. Mardi also has experience as a Domestic Violence Client Advocate, where she assisted both women and men in obtaining protective orders, relocating to safe shelters, and achieving divorce from their abusers.

With over 30 years of mediation experience in family, divorce, insurance, community, and EEOC cases across Canada and the United States, Mardi is currently recognized as a Credentialed Distinguished Mediator in Texas. She conducts mediation and communication training for various organizations. Mardi is an active member of several professional associations, including the AFCC, NADP, TAM, TMCA, CCE, and ICF. She is an ICF and BCC Executive and Leadership Coach, as well as a Certified Divorce Transition Coach. Mardi founded Positive Communication Systems, LLC, is a best-selling author, and hosts the podcast "The D Shift: Redefining Divorce and Beyond" and "Real Divorce Talks."

Connect with Mardi at www.divorcecoach4women.com.

CHAPTER 2
Was it My Fault?

Alana Sharps

I opened my eyes to find my husband looking down on me, jaw clenched, nostrils flared, with pupils dark, and dilated. He began to berate me again before pausing to say, "You're a vindictive bitch." I cringed in fear, backing away from him in the bed. His look of pure, visceral rage terrified me. My heart began to pound as if it wanted out of my chest. I tried to think of what to do to calm the situation. My palms dripped with sweat and no matter how many breaths I took; I couldn't get enough air. I panicked. *Is he going to hurt me?*

How did I get here?

Rewinding 12 years, I thought I had married the man of my dreams … my soulmate. I met my future husband in my mid-20s through an online dating app. Six years my junior, I had zero desire to pursue a relationship. However, his endless pursuit for my attention wore down my walls to let him in. Over time, I fell in love with his rugged looks, sincerity, and charming personality. He knew exactly what to say to make me feel like the most special woman in the world. I was floating on clouds, my stomach fluttered with butterflies in anticipation of seeing him throughout the weeks of dating. We shared similar beliefs, interests, and goals. I felt I was whole when I was with him, loved, accepted, and wanted. This was a feeling I had longed for up until this point in my life. When my "true" love asked to marry me after months of dating, I immediately said yes. I couldn't imagine being with anyone else.

My Wedding

As a little girl in pigtails, I used to dream about my wedding. It was one of my key goals in life. I envisioned the flower girls walking down the aisle in their frilly dresses and the ring bearer in his mini-tuxedo swinging the ring pillow as he raced down the aisle. I also envisioned my best girlfriends standing beside me, smiling in pure joy as they watched me recite my vows to the love of my life. My wedding day was a dream come true in June 2002.

Surrounded by family and friends, I was getting ready to marry my love. As I stood next to my fiancé, anxiously anticipating the reading of our vows, I felt a drip of sweat fall from my forehead onto my neatly written words of devotion on my 3x5 flashcard. I was nervous and excited at the same time. *"Don't mess up, don't mess up, DON'T MESS UP."* I kept telling myself. I didn't mess up and had the wedding I dreamed of in addition to the party of the year at my reception. I couldn't have asked for anything more.

After the festivities ended, my husband and I arrived at our hotel for the night. Exhausted from months of stress, planning, preparation, and the festivities of the day, I inadvertently fell asleep while my husband showered. Moments later, the covers were abruptly ripped off me as my husband angrily crawled into bed clearly upset with me. I was frozen in confusion by his behavior and didn't know what to do. Instead of being empathetic and understanding, he was angry and hostile. My husband began demanding sex enraged by the fact that I fell asleep.

Who is this man and where is the man I dated?

I was now meeting a man I didn't recognize. A complete stranger to me… that I had just married! I brushed off his behavior that night as stress from our wedding, giving him the benefit of the doubt.

Reality Set In

Slowly over time, that loving, charming, and considerate man I dated and fell in love with morphed into a psychological abuser. To the outside world and family, I was married to a charismatic man, but behind closed doors he demeaned and emotionally abused me. My husband became emotionally manipulative, controlling, and intimidating over the course of our marriage. He made me feel guilty for any and everything that went wrong in his life or made him feel devalued.

He began to demand all of my time and grew angry if he didn't receive it. Even if that time was spent with our children. I stopped doing activities with friends to please him. I began walking on eggshells, thinking about every action, and choosing my words carefully to avoid conflict. If I didn't do what he wanted, when he wanted, or how he wanted it done, I was belittled, berated, and called selfish. Whenever I expressed the things he was doing to me in the relationship that invalidated my feelings, he turned the conversation around to what I did to him.

It was always about him. His wants and his needs. He was never satisfied regardless of how much I tried to please him, and everything was continuously my fault.

Whenever I was sick and required medical attention, he would get angry with me, complaining he had to take me to urgent care or the ER, never showing any compassion for my well-being. Yet, he demanded I show empathy for him and take care of his every need. He also expected rewards and compliments for taking care of his children. If I decided to treat myself to a hair day or nail day (once a month), I was called a horrible mother for thinking of myself and leaving him to watch the children.

I hit my lowest point when my husband had an affair with one of his direct reports at work and decided I was trash to be discarded. An affair he blamed me for because he didn't feel "loved." His verbal abuse escalated to nightly rants in an attempt to force me into signing a separation agreement I didn't agree with. The agreement favored him and didn't take into consideration the need for adequate resources and care for the children. His demands for retribution meant I deserved no grace, consideration, or empathy. The view was clearly only from his lens.

I was distraught and frail from the loss of 11 pounds from my small-framed body during my husband's affair. I couldn't eat because my stomach was a rollercoaster, not knowing what each day would entail. I couldn't sleep because he kept me up all night ranting, and I couldn't think straight due to sleep deprivation. I threatened to call the police one night during one of his rages when he just wouldn't let up no matter how much I pled with him to stop. He told me he was wasting his time being with me. I served my purpose, and he was ready to move on.

When my husband's chosen mistress decided to end the affair and return to her husband, my husband mourned her departure for months, often crying in bed at night. Upon reflection of the affair and its impact on my psyche, the biggest disappointment for me was the fact that he told me he would NEVER have an affair. He convinced me completely that in his mind it was a horrible thing to do to someone.

When the affair ended, we chose to rekindle our marriage. Or at least that's what I believed we were doing. To turn the tables, my husband began to accuse me of cheating. He constantly complained about the number of texts and phone calls I received, to the point that I resorted to having my phone on vibrate. I began to call my family and friends during my commute to and from work to connect with the outside world. He checked my phone records and called back numbers on my phone that he didn't recognize. If I was five minutes late coming home from work, I was automatically accused of being with another man and kept up all night having a senseless argument over seeing a man that didn't exist.

What I didn't realize at the time was that I was being coercively controlled. The emotional manipulation, gaslighting, and fear of being harmed kept me in an invisible fence I was unable to escape. My cognitive dissonance between the belief that deep down my husband was a good man based on the man he was when we dated versus the person I was living with now, kept me entangled even more. If I did everything he requested and stopped doing what he complained about, I truly believed I would see the man I dated again, not realizing that the man I dated never existed. My personal fear of failure, my obligation as a wife based on societal norms, and the guilt of the possible mental impact to my children for breaking up my marriage kept me mentally and physically imprisoned.

The Aftermath

No one ever intentionally enters a marriage planning for divorce. The love and devotion we have for our partners on our wedding day brings elation and joy to the thought of a future with our soulmates. My wedding day was one of the happiest days of my life. I had married the man of my dreams and had a fabulous time celebrating with family and friends.

I lived in mental chaos for years trying to keep my marriage together until I looked at myself in the mirror one day and didn't recognize the woman I had become. I lost my identity. I lost myself conforming to a man who repeatedly emotionally and psychologically abused me.

After 16 years of this altered reality, I made the decision to leave the marriage, recognizing the home was not safe for myself or my children. I was once a strong, independent, ambitious woman who became mentally broken. I wanted a safe environment for my children; and I wanted "me" back.

Leaving my marriage was just as difficult as being in the marriage itself since my husband was determined to make it as difficult as possible for me to leave him.

Yet, I persevered.

The moment I stepped foot into my tiny two-bedroom apartment was life-altering. I closed my eyes as tears rolled down my face in joy, while I stood in silence enjoying the peacefulness of freedom.

Healing

As I collected my thoughts and cleared my head over the days that followed my leaving, I devised a plan to heal my mind, body, and spirit. It was as if I had an awakening and woke up from a 16-year coma, and I was in my 20s again. That's how much I had mentally dissociated in my marriage for survival.

I began to read and educate myself on the signs of coercive control, personality disorders, and psychological abuse. I never wanted to enter into another relationship similar to my marriage; therefore, I began seeing a trauma therapist and dedicated two years of my life to working on myself. I wanted to rediscover my likes, dislikes, and truly understand me. I gave up myself in my marriage to accommodate a man whose singular and sole purpose was to break my spirit.

I scheduled an appointment with a nutritionist and functional medicine doctor one week after I escaped my marriage to begin to heal my body from years of chronic stress. I also started an exercise plan to assist with my mental health and mood. I scheduled time with family and friends to reconnect and spend quality time. My friends and family became very important to me during this time as my support system. I needed their encouragement, their love, and for them to keep me accountable on my path to rediscovery and healing.

I began meditating before bed every night to clear my mind for restful sleep. I had been sleep deprived for so long that my body had grown accustomed to living in hypervigilance and chaos. It was difficult to calm my nervous system in the beginning to obtain the restful sleep I so desperately needed.

To rebuild my confidence and self-esteem that had become shattered during my marriage, I made a list of affirmations to state every morning and night. I also wrote a list of goals I wanted to accomplish over the next year as well as a list of activities I wanted to do over the next six months.

Post-Separation Abuse

After escaping my marriage, I thought that I was finally free from the emotional manipulation, control, and gaslighting. Little did I know or understand that I unknowingly stepped foot into post-separation abuse.

Many people think that abuse stops once you leave an abusive relationship; however, when you share children with your abuser, you encounter what is known as post-separation abuse. Post-separation abuse comes in the form of financial and legal abuse, harassment/stalking, using the children as pawns, etc.

Prior to moving out of the marital home, my soon-to-be ex-husband and I signed a separation agreement that not only entailed how we would split our assets, but how we would co-parent our children. A few months after I escaped the marital home, my co-parent filed for child custody citing parental alienation. I was very confused by this since our separation agreement clearly stated how we would handle child custody, and we were both adhering to the schedule. It wasn't until my 15-year-old daughter decided to not do overnight parental exchanges with her dad that child custody became a problem.

Instead of talking to his daughter about why she didn't want to spend time with him, he blamed me and accused me of parental alienation. I was devastated. Not knowing the family court system or how it worked, I had no idea how to fight his bogus and hurtful claims. I was confused and terrified of losing my kids. I didn't understand why we couldn't have a conversation instead of resorting to using the legal system — but when you're dealing with someone who wants to control everything and everyone around them including the narrative, it all makes sense.

Needless to say, co-parenting was another challenge I had to learn to navigate.

Since I was dealing with Complex Post Traumatic Stress Disorder (C-PTSD), every email, text, and phone call from my soon-to-be ex-husband triggered me. My palms would sweat, my hands would shake, and my heart would start pounding anticipating an attack due to my state of hypervigilance. Every form of communication either involved an attack on my character, a false accusation, or manipulation tactic to trigger me into an emotional response. I had to learn to respond to all communication in a calm manner without emotion.

Unfortunately, I learned this the hard way after being chastised by my attorney. Responding emotionally made me look bad and in turn, my soon-to-be ex-husband would use my responses as a form of evidence to support his narrative that I was the crazy mom who was unstable and unable to raise her kids. I did eventually learn the proper way to communicate, which also protected my mental health. No more verbal conversations or phone calls. All communication through written form only. You can't deny written communication, but you can deny a conversation. Since my co-parent was a pathological liar, written communication was definitely needed for my own protection.

My Children

On top of the co-parenting woes, my children were all in different stages of trauma. My goal was to help everyone heal by first providing them a safe environment free of ridicule, blame, gaslighting, and emotional and physical abuse. Secondly, we all needed therapy to heal from what we endured in the marital home. I was so caught up in my own survival while married, that I missed the signs of distress in my own children. I thought I was doing the right thing by keeping the family together when in reality, I was mentally hurting us all. My kids didn't open up about what their father did to them until we moved out of the home. Hearing their stories broke my heart into a million pieces.

"Mom guilt" set in and set me back on my healing journey. I had to get over the fact that I did the best I could, but I just couldn't get past the fact that I brought this man into our lives. Especially my oldest son who was almost two years old when I got married. He didn't deserve the inhumane treatment he experienced over my 16 years of marriage. Children just want to be loved, nurtured, seen, and heard. Not made to feel unworthy, unloved, inadequate, and a nuisance.

The Transformation

Looking back on those early days of dating, I was able to make the connection between my childhood feelings of not feeling loved, which allowed me to fall for my husband's charm and false persona of a loving and caring man. He knew exactly what to say to hook me into his web of deception and keep me there until I was locked into marriage.

Surviving my marriage and the post-separation abuse that followed led me to the study of Narcissistic Personality Disorder, Post Traumatic Stress Disorder, and how the family court system operates. I felt alone, overwhelmed, and stressed during my marriage and during the post-separation abuse that followed during my child custody battle. Due to my experience, I felt compelled to help others who are enduring the same trauma.

- People who may not realize they are in an abusive relationship.

- People who may not realize that emotional abuse is domestic abuse — a form of abuse that does not result in outward physical scars as our scars are hidden within our brains.

I am happy and fulfilled with my life now. My children and I are healing every day and rebuilding our lives. We are a family unit. We support, love, and deeply care for one another. My children are at peace and so am I.

Looking back on my past, I regret not leaving sooner. Fear, obligation, and guilt kept me locked into a situation I shouldn't have stayed in. I look forward to the day that I find that special someone, a person of integrity, who has empathy, compassion, and gives mutual respect. If I never find that someone, I'll still be happy, and content with the life I have.

Alana Sharps

Alana Sharps, founder of SurThrive Tribe, carries a wealth of experience as both a High Conflict Divorce and Child Custody Consultant and a Best-Selling Author. Her expertise extends beyond her professional achievements; it's rooted in her personal triumphs. Having navigated through the complexities of a toxic marriage entwined with psychological abuse, Alana emerged as a committed advocate for those facing similar trials. Her story is one of transformation — from a victim to an empowered survivor — and it fuels her dedication to guiding others through the challenging landscapes of domestic strife.

As an educator in the field of psychological abuse, Alana infuses her coaching with the same passion that drove her advocacy. Alana's unique perspective enhances her teachings, connecting the dots between psychology, human behavior, and personal experience. Her unwavering commitment to supporting others shines through in her approach to coaching, creating an enriching and supportive environment for her clients.

Alana is a graduate of North Carolina State University with a degree in Mechanical Engineering. She is also a Six Sigma enthusiast in process improvement and has coached numerous C-Suite executives, yielding millions in corporate-wide cost savings. Beyond her professional pursuits, Alana serves the community in several nonprofits. She is a board member for Time4Change of NC, a mentor to women in the HER Foundation, and a member of the National Society of Black Engineers.

Connect with Alana at https://www.surthrivetribe.com.

CHAPTER 3
It's All Mindset

Amy Danielle Taylor

I want to dedicate this chapter to my daughter Josie, my son Nic, my parents Linda and Barry, my sister Mary, and my two best friends, Tacy and Carolyn. They were all there for me and always have been.

Life's not perfect now. It wasn't perfect before my marriage or during my marriage, so why would it be after my divorce? However, life is more peaceful, and I am much happier than I was pre-divorce. I learned so much from my marriage and my divorce. There are many things I would have done differently, looking back now. I try not to look back much anymore, though.

I try to focus on the here and now. I have goals and dreams again and I am working towards them on a daily basis. I made some tough choices due to finances and moved back in with my parents for five years. My ex-husband made fun of me for not being able to take care of myself and living with my "Mommy" and "Daddy." But what he didn't know, and didn't need to know, was that I was paying my parents a small amount to live there and then saving the rest to buy a house. I was also working with a company to fix my credit and get a great deal on my house. Was it easy? Nope. Was it worth it? YEP! I'm still living in the beautiful home I bought eight years ago. My daughter and I love it here.

I was also told by my ex that I would get fired from my new job in a few months or less. It's almost 12 years later, and I'm just now leaving that company on my own accord to move into a better position with a new company. Not only did I keep my job, I went back to grad school and got my MBA. I've done a lot of great things since getting divorced. I took my daughter to Disney World and bought beautiful furniture for my home (not right away, but when I could, as I could). I've spent time with friends and family without feeling like I was taking time away from him or getting guilt tripped about it from him. There was no more getting gaslighted while he slept with other women and made me feel like the one who was ruining everything.

I finally feel at peace and have for many years now. It didn't happen quickly as I was still angry when I moved into my new home eight years ago. It took me about six years to realize that my anger only fueled the bitterness and unhappiness and set a bad example for my daughter. Ultimately, I didn't want to feel that way, so I forgave him for everything.

Well, I didn't tell him that, but I forgave him. My daughter loves him, so no matter how I feel about him not seeing her enough or not knowing her very well at all, it doesn't help me (or her) to focus on those negative things. Instead, I just remember that she loves him and that's what matters. I treat him with respect because she should see me doing that. I am ashamed to say that that wasn't always the case.

It's not about how low we go; it's about how high we rise. I realized to be happy again I not only had to forgive him, but I had to move on with my life. I personally haven't dated much because I decided to focus on my daughter (who is on the spectrum and takes some extra attention and focus from me). I take her to her psychiatry and therapy appointments and work with the schools and do whatever it takes to care for her.

I am in love with my life now. Not every day is great, but a lot of them are. It's not about being happy all the time. It's about recognizing the little things and being happy whenever you can be. I enjoy my life now.

I finally came to the realization that life was much better on my own. I have the freedom to do what I want, when I want, and I don't ever have to feel bad about my choices. How is he doing? Is he dating anyone? Is he happy? I don't know. I don't care. Well, actually, I hope he is happy as I wouldn't wish unhappiness on anyone, and the happier he is, the nicer he will be to our daughter when he does see her.

I didn't have any control of the money before. As soon as I was paid, I had to turn over my checks to him. I wasn't even allowed to buy clothes for our daughter from the Salvation Army thrift store when hers were all too tight and no longer weather appropriate. I remember one time when I was brave and cashed my check. I took my daughter to The Salvation Army thrift store and bought her a handful of appropriate clothing that fit better. Boy, was he angry with me. I remember feeling like the worst mother and the worst wife all at the same time.

Now, I do my own budgeting. Do I always do it perfectly? No, but it's always my choices and decisions I have to live with, and I will always put my child first.

I also remember when we first divorced and he was actually seeing her occasionally on alternating weekends and sometimes on Wednesday for dinner. I was still the one taking care of her full time and bringing her to daycare every day. She loved routines and later we found out why— her being on the Autism spectrum. So, when it was Daddy & Donuts Day, I showed up at the daycare with our daughter and he showed up to walk inside with her to have donuts. When it was time for this little two-year-old to switch hands, she went ballistic. She began screaming and crying like somebody was hurting her. That made him very angry, so he left. I ended up bringing her into Daddy & Donuts Day and she calmed right down. He, of course, thought I was telling our daughter horrible things about him, thereby making her scared of him. I asked him then as I'll ask you now, "Why would I do that to a little girl when she needs her Daddy?" Little girls need to be loved by their dads so they aren't seeking out the wrong attention later in life to fill that void inside of them.

If I could tell divorcing parents anything, it would be to be kind to each other at least in front of the children and never speak of the other parent negatively in front of them. In fact, I know from my own childhood experience that when one parent bad mouths the other parent, it is the parent doing the badmouthing that the child feels resentment towards later. Children should be allowed to love their parents with their whole heart and never have that questioned.

Another thing I learned is to give up the picture of the perfect family, whatever that is, and to make your little family perfect for you and your children. That includes whatever the other parent wants to contribute. I tried for so long to make my ex-husband see our daughter regularly and tried to get him to pay his child support on time and tried to get him to pay for his half of the medical bills, etc.

I finally realized that I am not his boss, and I don't even want to be his boss. It's too time consuming and emotionally exhausting.

When I decided to let him be the dad he wanted to be, then everything became easier. I paid the bills with what money I had until child support took the money from him. I quit asking him to pay his half of the medical bills because it was obvious he wasn't going to and I was just giving myself extra anxiety trying to get him to do something he wasn't going to do. The only one suffering was me. He didn't care. Why should I? Did I have to come up with more money? Yes, but I did what I had to do and I quit trying to control someone I could never control anyway. When you finally decide to let your ex just be themselves and you quit trying to make them into the image you have in your head, life becomes so much simpler and you feel more calm.

Ultimately, when you realize that your primary responsibility is to yourself and your child or children, everything becomes clearer. You know exactly what you need to do, let go of concerns about your ex, and allow them to be who they have always been.

Since that revelation, life has been so much better. I feel much freer as I only have to control myself and my reactions. Am I always perfect when responding to my ex, no, but I'm much better than I was and I improve as time and distance make room for me to do so.

I realize now that I can't even control my child. I can only encourage and guide. My child is her own little person and will have to control herself with my help, as needed.

Now that I only have to control myself and my life, I'm free to dream up all that's possible. I get to decide where to work, how to spend my money, where I live, where I go on vacation, etc. I realize there are times when the divorce decree says that you have to live in a certain area close to your child's other parent, or you have to share time 50/50 so you can never get too far, but even that can be survived and made better.

I've always felt this way, but I cried and cried when I was granted 50/50 custody and learned that my daughter would be with me four days a week and her dad three days a week, with alternating holidays. However, as it turned out, my ex didn't want to follow that arrangement. He told me he would just take her every other weekend and Wednesday nights, which soon dwindled to only every other weekend, and eventually to rare visits. Despite living only 10 miles away, he became more distant, and during Covid, he didn't see her at all for two years.

I soon realized I had all the decision-making power as her parent as he began to ignore my requests for his input and he didn't show up at any school conferences or to any medical appointments. At first, I was mad because, again, I was trying to make him be what I thought was the perfect dad. But then I turned it all around in my head and realized I had all the decision-making power and he wanted it that way and I wanted it that way and she was happy as a bee in a bonnet. So, why had I been complaining at all? You see, it's all from your perspective of things. You get to decide whether something is negative or positive and only you can switch a negative to a positive.

Since my divorce, I have truly taken the time to read and listen to a load of self-help books and tried therapy again and again and talked my mom's and friend's ears off getting to the point I am today. Please don't be upset if you are angry and jealous or whatever you might be feeling in the first part of the divorce. As I said, it took me six years to really get my head on straight and realize this was my life to live the way I wanted to live it and I didn't want to spend another second thinking about my ex in any way more than I absolutely had to.

If you are one of the really lucky ones who has a great relationship with your ex and get along swimmingly, then yay!!! That is something to truly be thankful for. And if your ex does half of the parenting and you get to rest sometimes, then yay, enjoy that free time. But just know if you are not given the luxury of a super friendly and loving relationship with your ex and/or your ex doesn't want to actually do half or any of the parenting with you, well, just know that is not condemning you to an unhappy life. Being a single parent is rough, but it is also wonderful. I don't argue in front of the kids with some other adult. I don't waste time trying to make decisions with the other adult as I do what I think is right and then make it work.

Some people decide they are not going to date while raising their children, especially if they have special needs like my child. You may be wondering how you will survive being lonely. Well, that is up to you. In the beginning, I was very lonely. I thought I would never stop feeling so alone, especially at night and especially when my friends and family were busy and my child was sleeping. When I had too much time on my hands, it was hard. I cried and felt down and out. But, when I made that pivotal decision to start focusing on what I can control in my life, that changed too.

I finally realized that being happy or lonely and sad all depended on how I looked at things. I realized that when my child was sleeping and I was actually still awake and lonely that was because I was choosing to be lonely. I could value my free time and watch a show or read a book or work on getting my MBA and I did all of those things. I soon looked forward to nights to indulge in my desires. I realized that when you are happy with yourself and your life then you don't feel so lonely. I have learned to treasure my alone time. My daughter is now 14 and I have a lot of alone time as she holes up in her room, doing her thing and ignoring me, lol (teens will be teens). I enjoy being able to have some silence and be alone with my thoughts and figure out what I want to do next and then take action to start doing that thing.

What I want to impart on you is that divorce doesn't have to be the end! It can be the beginning! I feel so lucky that I finally figured it out and quit wallowing around in my own muck. I took control back and took charge of my life and now I am in a much better place, financially, emotionally, educationally, and I've built a great inner relationship with myself and great relationships with my children.

It may sound like I'm advocating for everyone to go it alone and not get into the dating world again. That is not the case. I don't think anyone else needs to do that just because I decided it would make me happier. I made that choice for many reasons and I'm glad I did, but I know other divorced women who got right back in the dating scene and ended up re-married soon after and are still married all these years later and are happy as well. I don't care whether you decide to be a single parent, co-parent with your ex, or find someone new to help co-parent, just as long as you realize you are the one in control of your life. And I think it's important to love yourself as much as you love anyone else, even your child. That is vital, not only so you will be happy, but so you're modeling that self-love for your children.

Not everything I try works. I tried to run my own business and after a year decided to give up on that. However, I still had fun learning how to run a business and am not sorry for the time I put into it at all. I also started a podcast about mental health and neurodiversity. After all, who better to host a podcast on mental health and neurodiversity than a single mom who has bipolar disorder and ADHD with a daughter who is on the autism spectrum with ADHD. My grown son also has ADHD, so I am well versed on the subject. I've had so much fun interviewing people and have learned so very much about the different ways to help people. If you think that might be something you're interested in, please feel free to check out my podcast on all major podcasting platforms under "Advancing With Amy / Mental Health Warrior & Neurospicy Mama."

No matter what, I hope you can take something out of this chapter, even if it's just how important it is to love and take control of yourself and stop trying to control everyone else. Remember how short life is and that you only have one chance to become who you want to be. Make yourself the best version of you that you can imagine and be proud of who you are.

And if this is all just the beginning for you, remember that I didn't come to this positive realization overnight. Don't be too hard on yourself if you don't either. Take time to grieve the loss of a marriage, the loss of the life you saw together, and be angry if you need to be angry and be sad if you need to be sad. Just remember how short life is and live it now while you still can!

Amy Danielle Taylor

Amy Danielle Taylor is a social worker of almost 30 years and a recent 2024 MBA graduate. She is the host of Advancing With Amy / Mental Health Warrior & Neurospicy Mama, a podcast about mental health and neurodiversity.

Amy is a single Mom of two only children as she had her kiddos 18 years apart. She has one daughter, one son, one daughter-in-law and three grandchildren. She looks forward to whatever life brings her next.

Connect with Amy at www.advancingwithamy.com.

CHAPTER 4

Loving My Son More
Than Taking Revenge

Christina Sabine Synnott

To Anyone Going Through Divorce...

As I drove past the authentic British pub in the picturesque village of Markham, Ontario, last Tuesday, it all came rushing back to me, how it started: the idea of joint custody.

Back in the fall of 1990, my husband and I had dinner at that same pub and the topic of how parents divide up their children when divorcing came up. We were still hanging on and trying, but our marriage was on very shaky ground.

The recently released movie, 'Kramer vs. Kramer' with Meryl Streep and Dustin Hoffman had frightened me badly (as well as probably the rest of the world) at how cruelly divorce could affect a formerly normal and happy child.

Horror stories from my wonderful Italian hairdresser, Ray, just exacerbated my fears. He told me that each time he went to pick up his mini-me lookalike eight-year-old son for an outing, his ex-wife would hold out her hand and demand $100 cash … just to visit his own son. I was appalled at the very thought of it. The real kicker happened, though, when Ray arrived one summer evening at his ex-wife's house in downtown Toronto to pick up sweet Mario, now 10 years old, for their annual father and son holiday week at my cottage in Muskoka. After Ray rang the doorbell of his former home, his mother-in-law answered and promptly informed him that his ex-wife had taken Mario to Disneyland in Florida … for Ray's highly anticipated, previously scheduled week. Ah, revenge! I am certain she would have felt great satisfaction watching Ray stumble back alone to his van loaded with fishing tackle, lake toys, and groceries for the BBQ, as tears streamed down his cheeks.

So, when my husband and I were sitting in the Markham pub, I shared Ray's story and told him about 'Kramer vs. Kramer,' and asked, "Can we please agree on something? If we were ever to separate or divorce, could we please try joint custody to protect our son, Jamie, as much as possible?" I continued, "It will be difficult losing his parents together as a unit and a shared home, but at least he would know that he was loved by both parents." We agreed!

Later, hearing stories of Princess Diana of Wales and other children of divorce who lost one parent, I knew I made the correct decision. As far as I could tell from Princess Diana's memoirs, she believed that her mother had walked away and abandoned her. As a child, she was unaware that her mother had fought hard in court to gain minimal visitation rights, but to a child that means little. It usually results in children thinking that the parent who left or who they rarely saw doesn't love them. I doubt that is the case most times. I had the unusual belief that as long as one of the parents was not an axe murderer, a child would probably develop better knowing that both Mom and Dad loved them. Of course, I would've also enjoyed some revenge and to get even, but at what cost? The price would mean my son's unhappiness at missing his dad and quite likely it would result in damaging his self-esteem.

This was not an easy decision for me. One year after our pub discussion, the inevitable happened, we were living separately, awaiting our divorce. In the early 1990s, divorce was not cool (not that it is cool today, but it's become the norm and is more accepted). I didn't have any support. As a matter of fact, my father told me I was stupid for divorcing, I lost most of my friends and, believe it or not, people truly imagined divorce was a contagious disease which might spread to their marriage, so a divorcée became like a leper.

When I questioned former girlfriends why we couldn't hang out anymore, they unanimously responded, "Now that you are single, you might want to take our husbands." I laughed at the absurdity, tried to assure them I had zero interest in their spouses (let alone any man at that time), but they were gone. Thank God I had a job and my own car given to me by my father – a 20-year-old hand-me-down family red Mercedes.

Although living in a big city like Toronto with excellent public transportation does make it possible for a single parent to get around, I imagine without a daily purpose and income, it would be extremely difficult to leave a marriage.

At night, on the far side of our shared king-sized bed, I planned and plotted how to get away. I had already tried to escape once two years earlier, after a particularly bitter fight whereby my elbow was repeatedly smashed into the inside of our heavy wooden front door. I had to finally admit that my husband had not 'disappeared' as I had always convinced myself. He was perfectly aware of what he had done and didn't even apologize afterwards.

Since my dad had beaten me as a child, I didn't like it, but it was familiar. It only got worse when I asserted myself and stated to my husband, "I am your equal partner. You cannot speak to me like that." Boof! During this incident, my two-year-old son was in his baby carrier and began crying profusely, sensing something was wrong. My husband threw me across the room (usually at night) causing black and blue bruises at least twice a year during our 10-year marriage, but this time it affected our son, so I immediately drove my car from the garage to the driveway, ran upstairs to pack a small bag of clothes, grabbed my son in his carrier, and walked out the front door.

On the porch stood my 6'4" husband (I'm only 5'4" tall) who easily pulled the carrier out of my hands, exclaiming, "You can go, but without Jamie." Oh, no! I imagined the courts condemning me as a neglectful mother, leaving my son behind until I could figure out an alternate way to get him back. Back in in the 1990s, calling the police and charging your husband with spousal abuse in front of the entire neighbourhood on a Sunday afternoon was out of the question. As a matter of fact, an abused woman did not even tell her mother, sisters, or friends because she was too ashamed of the man whom she had chosen. I lived by the old adages, "You made your bed, now lie in it" and "Until death do us part" and suffered in silence all alone.

Even now I am ashamed to admit that it took me two more years to get up the courage again to leave; therefore, the plotting at bedtime.

As I lay on my side of the bed, questions arose such as:

- Can I get my son to daycare early enough, but also make it to work on time?

- What about having to work the long hours required in the hospitality industry and not being able to pick up my son before daycare closes?

To solve the latter issue, I hired my wonderful Italian neighbour, Connie, to pick up Jamie from daycare and feed him a snack until I could get there after a 10-hour workday plus a 2-hour commute, with many a dinner spent in a Wendy's drive-through.

After I solved this crucial working mother challenge, I welled up all my courage and very quietly from the far side of our bedroom told my husband that he had anger issues and he needed to get help. I handed him a telephone number and reiterated that 'he' must make the phone call. Fortunately, one day earlier, I had heard a talk show on the radio discussing precisely our predicament, which ended up saving all of us. The knowledgeable speaker spelled it out very clearly: If boys see an abusive father, they will themselves repeat what they saw and most likely abuse women too because it's how they learned to deal with anger. Just like me, if girls experienced or saw abuse in their childhood home, they will most likely choose an abusive partner.

"NO," I screamed. I did not want my sweet boy hurting his future wife and also living in an abusive marriage. "It is my responsibility as an adult and as his mother to prevent this...regardless of what happens to me," I thought. I loved Jamie enough. Actually, after the year we spent at Sick Kids Hospital in Toronto where Jamie, at a mere three years old, almost lost his kidney, I was a ferocious lioness. It was abundantly clear to me that I would never survive losing Jamie. Therefore, I would do anything necessary to protect my son.

After several months of me and my husband attending anger management sessions at Toronto's Insane Asylum (why I had to attend is still a puzzle to me), simultaneously with marital counselling, I knew that the trust between us was too badly broken and ultimately confirmed to my husband that our marriage was over.

He didn't want to move out of our basement nanny suite in our shared home, so I spent many weekends apartment hunting...for him.

Finally, I found a lovely apartment in a brand-new high rise building nearby, overlooking Lake Ontario with a small extra bedroom nook for Jamie. Unfortunately, this is when my husband decided that he still wanted me back and began stalking me, even threatening to jump from his 14th floor balcony if I didn't take him back. I looked at the drop from the balcony and, despite my profound former love for him, felt nothing anymore and said, "Go ahead!"

You may be wondering, "How could she in good conscience leave her son with such an abusive man?" I always knew that my Ex's anger was triggered by a power struggle between two adults. He needed to control a calm, subservient wife who would OBEY and that sure as hell wasn't me; an adventurous, brave, independent woman. Therefore, I was quite certain that my Ex-husband would never raise a hand to our boy and that was indeed the case. That's why I agreed to joint custody.

Custody Agreement

How did our custody agreement work? Strangely enough, in 1991 there were no real joint custody laws, so my lawyer had to thoroughly research to incorporate joint custody into our divorce agreement. Scheduling time with a parent or apart was difficult. Since Jamie was only a four-year-old toddler, neither of us could fathom being without him for more than a few days at a time. Therefore, we chose three days on, three days off, and every other weekend. In the beginning, the shuffling back and forth made Jamie crazy, but we didn't know a better solution. My Ex and I held weekly phone calls negotiating our son's health, food, schooling, and upcoming events until Jamie graduated from high school. Eventually, the three of us parents (including my Ex-husband's new wife) attended most of Jamie's activities whether it was a baseball tournament, a school function, or a hockey game. We didn't always sit together, but we were all there to show our support.

At first, life after divorce was difficult. It felt as if someone had placed me in a washing machine; spat me out; and then said, "Walk." The first three days after my Ex-husband moved out, I rocked back and forth in a rocking chair. That actually finally helped me acknowledge to myself that both my dad and husband had abused me. I knew I needed help and immediately made an appointment to see a therapist to try to find myself and spirit again since my self-esteem was completely gone. I felt like the dust bunny under the carpet. I was a frightened woman and was certainly terrified of all men. I could not be alone in an elevator with a man and that led to me taking self-defence classes so I would feel safer and be able to go back out into the world.

Then, I remembered that as a teen gaining her confidence, I used to swim competitively and downhill ski race, so I joined the Masters Group at Blue Mountain Ski Hill where young adults who had a day job raced slalom on the mountain on weekends. I could ski 55 kmph and that really helped me build back my confidence. Despite my Ex-husband's taunts that I couldn't do it, I became a Catering Manager at a posh hotel, The Westin Prince Hotel in Toronto, and was later promoted to Wedding Planner, organizing almost 60 weddings.

As a career single mom, I expected Jamie to help around the house. On the fridge was a list of weekly chores for him, which included walking our dog, shoveling snow, raking leaves, vacuuming, washing floors, doing his own laundry, and cooking at least one meal per week. I told Jamie that after the household chores were completed, we could go and have fun. Most Friday nights we went to the cinema to enjoy a movie together until he was a teenager and we both loved dining at the Rainforest Cafe beforehand. Living in the Beaches area of Toronto, we frequently bicycled or rollerbladed on the Boardwalk in the evenings. Every Mother's Day Jamie and I rollerbladed the entire length of Centre Island to our secret cafe for lemonade and cake. When Jamie asked for his own telephone, his own computer, and his own television, I laughed and replied, "We can certainly share the phone and computer and negotiate TV programming. If there is any money left over, I will show you the world," which I did.

The Challenges of Joint Parenting

Joint parenting was not always easy. I spent most of Jamie's first Christmas apart, crying on the kitchen floor because he was still only five years old. Stupidly, later, at Jamie's Grade 8 Public School graduation, I sat with my Ex and his wife, neglecting to bring along a friend to accompany me. As I happily gushed on about how dressed up and cute Jamie's friends looked because I knew them well, both Jamie's dad and Stepmom stared straight ahead not responding, as if I was invisible. I ran to the Lady's room to cry, realizing that I had no one to share my parenting joy with.

On one of my solo trips to Peru to learn Spanish, I began falling in love with my Spanish professor, Marciel, but Jamie was only 15 years old, so I returned home, leaving behind the possibility of that relationship. I had been single for over ten years and yearned for a relationship.

Fortunately, my Ex-husband comprehended the valuable world view which our son might acquire from travel. So when Jamie was 14 years old, my Ex agreed to let him join me as a volunteer in Ghana, Africa, where I was teaching Kindergarten for a non-profit organization. I am certain this experience led to Jamie studying international development at university, earning his Masters degree in International Relations at Groningen University in Holland, and his current job with a think-tank affiliated with the EU parliament in Brussels, doing amazing human rights work.

After a safari holiday in Kenya and Tanzania in 1997, I fell in love with Africa and began planning how I could manage hotels there in the future. In 2000, after Jamie and I had completed our volunteer work in Ghana, we spent a few days vacationing in Zanzibar, still the most exotic place in the world I have ever visited. I begged Jamie to stay there with me and attend the international school, but he missed his dad and friends too much. It also would have violated our joint custody agreement whereby we had promised to live within one hour of one another for mutual access to our son.

As the ferry slid away from Zanzibar, tears running down my cheeks, we made a four-year pact. I promised that I would take on mediocre jobs in Toronto for the next few years while Jamie completed his entire high school curriculum, but immediately after that, I would return to Africa to advance my career, managing hotels there. I'm certain that Jamie thought I was kidding until I ordered a limousine for his high school graduation party and then the next day flew to Kenya to manage a hotel in the seaside resort town of Diani Beach. My former close friends and cottage neighbours accused me of abandoning my son and running off to Africa, but Jamie was going off to university only one and a half hours from his dad's home in Ontario. I found it very odd because at 18 years of age, I had moved to Austria to study Hotel Management at Salzburg University without knowing anyone there. I thought that's what students did to become independent adults.

When Jamie was in university, every six months I flew him to wherever I was working and he was fortunate enough to partake in incredible adventures with me. The night before Jamie climbed Mt. Kilimanjaro in Tanzania, he told me how proud he was that I had followed my dreams and had shown him a good example to aspire to. He assured me that he was glad that I had left him alone at university to grow up and become a man and to learn how to solve his own challenges. And of course he knew that both his dad and I were only a phone call away.

Through all these shared adventures and spending large amounts of quality time together, Jamie and I grew very close. I consider him to be not only my son and my best friend, but one of the best human beings I have ever met with a huge, caring heart.

I have managed many small hotels all over the world and published a book, *Tales of a Gypsy Hotelier*, but I consider my very greatest accomplishment that Jamie broke two generations of abuse and married the most loving equal partner. In hindsight, I realize we gave Jamie a huge gift by divorcing, so that he would not emulate our unhappy, fighting, and abusive relationship, thereby making a much better choice.

I went from being a survivor of divorce and abuse, all the way to building my own successful boutique hotel on the Namibian coast of Africa. For that, I'm grateful I followed my heart.

Christina Synnott

Christina Synnott was born and grew up in nature, a village in Northern Ontario, Canada, along one of the great lakes. After graduating from Brentwood College on Vancouver Island, BC, she earned a Bachelor degree in Hotel & Tourism Management at Schloss Klessheim, affiliated with the University of Salzburg, in Austria. She deliberately chose this prestigious hotel school so she could participate in the apprenticeship program, working as a chamber maid: waitress; in the Garde Manger of the Kitchen; and later, as Front Desk Receptionist at the world-renowned Hotel Traube Tonbach, in the Black Forest, in Germany.

Christina also earned a Diploma in Hotel Sales from Cornell University in Ithaca, New York, and a subsequent Certificate in Marketing & Advertising from Ryerson University in Toronto.

After working her way up through several hotels in Toronto (including the Fairmont Royal York and Westin Prince Hotel) and after her first safari to Africa, Christina began managing hotels throughout Africa, in St. Lucia (Caribbean), and in Tonga (South Pacific).

During a tourism recession, Christina wrote and published a travel memoir, *Tales of a Gypsy Hotelier*, in a hut on an out-island in Fiji.

In 2017, 'Villa Maji' (house on the water in Swahili), her 23-year-long dream of owning a small hotel in Africa, was born on the coast of Namibia and ran successfully for many years.

Christina has now returned home to Muskoka, Canada, with her African rescue dog, Snoopy, working as a Hotel Consultant and Writer. She also loves to paint.

Connect with Christina at www.gypsyphotelier.com and

synnott_chri@protonmail.com.

CHAPTER 5

Is There a Healthy Other Side of Divorce for Kids?

Dinalynn Rosenbush

This chapter is dedicated to Gwen, Emma, and Cole who struggled with me and we became resilient. I am so proud to be your mother! I love you!

This book is designed to help you see the future possibility and to be encouraged for yourself and for your kids. There is another side of divorce for kids. We create it.

When I first divorced, I wondered if there was another side, *especially for my kids.* Sometimes, divorce sets kids free from danger so that they can become well and healthy. Sometimes, it is only loss and confusion. For many, the divorce becomes a defining moment both positive and negative. Let's look at the positives of what can be possible.

When done well, your kids become well. Since we all come to divorce for different reasons, let's look at common success traits to adapt and thrive and how we help our kids get to a space of peace, calm, and love.

We all want our kids to be emotionally regulated. Emotional regulation is the ability to manage and respond to emotional experiences in a healthy and balanced way. Children who develop strong emotional regulation skills can manage the ups and downs of life more effectively, making it easier for them to cope with stressful situations, such as those brought on by divorce. It helps them maintain emotional balance, prevent outbursts, and recover more quickly from emotional setbacks. Sounds great, huh?!

Sounds like a great skill for *adults* you know?

Exactly! That is the key!

This growth doesn't happen spontaneously nor because of the divorce. Rather, learning to regulate oneself is a choice. Your kids need to see examples of people managing their emotions well. A divorce is a prime pressure cooker for experiencing the biggest of emotions – as you well know! Which means, you are in a prime place to demonstrate and teach your children!

This leads us to the tricky part! When you are at max capacity, you may not do it well.

Therefore, you start with a different part. You start where you are. That is… owning your behavior and learning to forgive.

You may think you already do this. Chances are, you could get better. I know this because when I got a divorce, I was much less "glued" to myself than I am today. The healthy Other Side of Divorce for ME included becoming **more grounded.**

One healthy other side of divorce for my KIDS was the ability to **trust, forgive, and apologize well**.

The first thing I needed to learn was to apologize to my kids often. When I was snippy, unnecessarily hurried, easily frustrated, or otherwise impatient with them, I had to apologize. I realized that I was short with my children for acting like children! (*Not fair!*) I was irritated because I was spent and viewed their behavior as too slow, too fast, too messy… In other words, I felt out of control, so I tried to create a smooth, controlled home life. That didn't work. I needed to let them be who they are. I learned to forgive myself for my imposed self-judgments and behaviors that were me not being the parent I wanted to be. I learned to forgive them for not doing things "right" – which really meant "My Way."

So, what is forgiveness anyway?

I now define forgiveness as *"letting go of my right to be ____ (angry, resentful, bitter, etc…)"*

Notice that ...

I am Not saying that I should not feel.

I am Not saying what someone did was right.

I am Not saying anything about fairness or right-ness.

We have the right to be angry! How long you choose to stay angry is a choice. Being angry over time harms you and those you love. Plus, your anger does not hurt the person you are angry at! It only fuels the separation. It is wisdom to let go of anger when no further good comes from it.

The second thing I needed to do was learn to make a good apology. There are parts to an apology that make it strong enough to really connect to the heart of the person we are apologizing to. Kids feel when an apology is partial or inauthentic.

Your good apology needs to acknowledge:

(1) the impact of your actions,

(2) owning your part in the problem,

(3) expressing regret or sorrow,

(4) an offer to make amends.

Of course this must be done in the context of really **listening**. No correction, teaching, or defense! Your kids will often want to say their side of the story. They won't believe your apology if they don't feel heard or you won't accept what they say about the situation. It takes some practice and skill to be able to listen well when you disagree.

Then, ask them, "What did you hear me say?" I learned that I cannot assume they really got it! Sometimes our kids can't process what we say because they have their own big feelings going on. An apology isn't very helpful when it isn't understood well!

True forgiveness and authentic apologies anchor our kids in their trust for us no matter their age.

When I got divorced, I believed that the world outside of me "made me feel" this way or that. The healthy Other side of Divorce for me was realizing that Happiness is an Inside Job! I am actually in control of what feelings I feel. Plus, the feelings I feel are a response to how I _view_ what is going on. This means that when I change my thinking, I change my feelings. When I change my feelings, I change my life.

This understanding is part of **Boundaries**. I define boundaries as "knowing what you are responsible for and what you are not" (adapted from Townsend and Cloud's book, *Boundaries*). Kids need to learn that they are responsible for what they think, feel, do, and say. Plus, they can learn to control what they think, feel, do, and say. The tricky part is that often parents and kids are learning this together! That was the case for me as well!

Grace! Be gracious with your kids and yourself! Your kids follow you.

Your kids can be **well-adjusted humans,** able to regulate their emotions and able to navigate daily challenges without being overwhelmed by their feelings.

Sounds too good to be true? If you are thinking, *"I can't even do that,"* you are not alone. Lots of us learn alongside our kids! This is why I started this chapter with learning to apologize, forgive, and have lots and lots of grace! This is a process that continues as long as you are focused on growing. A simple description is to have the ability to express feelings in a healthy way and to have the ability to cope with stress and painful feelings.

Let's look at a few ways that emotionally regulated people interact.

Conversations About Their Feelings

Oftentimes, happy, sad, mad, and glad are the main working vocabulary we use. You and your children are experiencing more emotions than that. Learning to use specific, emotional vocabulary to match your feelings is a powerful blend of building connection and identifying the truth within yourself. Empowerment occurs for all of you as you are drawn closer. Remember that your response and interpretation will be very different from your child's response and interpretation of the same situation. Therefore, honor their experience by listening without judgment or opinion as they share their feelings.

I learned that emotionally regulated people have conversations with a *"play mindset."*

Here is what that looks like.

Take a breath, relax, and read the following words. Think about how EACH. WORD. FEELS. in your body and read one-by-one.

Exploration. Curiosity. Discovery. Awe. Try-New-Things. Brave. Doing. Challenge. Wonder. Enjoyment. Design. Fun. Practice. Creativity. Develop. Experiment. Adventure. Fascination. Imagination. Joy. Become.

When you mentally shift into this brain space, you have entered PLAY. Communicate with your kids this way! When your kids are expressing tough feelings with poor behaviors, you can lean into the words: *exploration, discovery, wonder* as you slowly, gently, uncover what is going on FOR THEM - INSIDE THEM.

***Tip:** It is really helpful for your kids if you label your feelings, so they see it done. However, your details about your ex should be saved for a friend or counselor, and not expressed when kids are around. Therefore, express feelings about other areas of life. Don't forget gratitude and positive feelings!*

Let's consider HOW to have conversations about THEIR feelings using the words above!

First, become an example, using many feeling words in your daily speech.

Second, you need to pause, remember, and explore.

*Hold that mental shift into the space of discovery, exploration, and wonder as you uncover what is going on. Along the way, you slip in emotional **vocabulary.**

Let's use a normal, common example: Your child has just pushed his brother down and knocked a plant pot over. The natural reaction is to stop him and scold him.

What if …

… you remembered that he did not sleep well last night?

… you paused to think about what happened for him recently?

… you remembered that his plans for today were canceled?

And THEN, you approached him using language of play around discovery, exploration, and curiosity.

"You seem angry today."

[No, I'm not!] Ignore their defense.

"I remember that today you were going to go to Joe's house, but that was canceled." (your long, quiet pause usually makes kids naturally begin talking).

"If that happened to me, I would feel disappointed. Do you feel disappointed?" (long, quiet pause, allow him to agree or disagree, you listen and validate the feeling).

"What would help you feel better today?" (long, quiet pause, come alongside. Be on his team.).

In this case, you gave your child space and time to process and talk by listening. You paused, remembered, and explored what might be going on for him. You gave him vocabulary and power to say if that vocabulary was correct. You came alongside with support and encouragement. Good Job!

This helped your child's anger become more specific. You learned that disappointment is his actual feeling. We respond differently to disappointment than meanness, so let's interpret playfully, exploring what may be true for our kids. The end result is that your child feels seen, heard, and validated. We ALL respond differently when we feel seen, heard, and validated.

***Tip:** It should be noted that when we ask our kids what is going on, they often say "nothing" or "I don't know." This is often true. They often don't know in those moments. They answer this way because they are not aware yet of their own thoughts and feelings (btw ~ true for many adults, too). Words offered to match their experience helps our kids grow their vocabulary.*

How we talk to ourselves about ourselves matters. Your healing and growth will be evident as you use exploration, gentleness, joy, and kindness in the words you say to yourself. It's tough to change this on your own, so get help.

Coping Strategies

Coping strategies allow us to manage intensity and choose our responses. Whichever coping strategies you use, let your child see it! When you emerge composed after hiding in the bathroom, engage in deep breathing, meditation, or get some exercise. This allows your children to see how it is done. It shows them directly what you are doing to better manage your big feelings.

As I was in the process of divorce, I was filled with anger and had lots of anger-energy to go along with it. This is one area where I did fairly well. I ran a mile – as fast as I could. I did this a couple of times a day. I was gone 8-10 minutes each time. I said to my children, *"I am mad. I am going on a run so that I can feel better. I love you."* That was about it! They saw this repeatedly. It helped me to be in a better state of mind so that I could be a better parent. I got in pretty good shape!

What will work for you?

Enter a Play Mindset as with the kids. Be kind. Be gentle. The child inside of you needs this. Explore and try something new! Find enjoyment. Find Release. Be brave and uncover your ways to heal. I learned to use breathwork, meditation, reframing, along with creative activities. Many of these can be done with kids, exposing them to a variety of self-supportive strategies.

Joy of Learning!

This is a direct outcome of adopting what I call a "Play Mindset." In order to learn, you need to be relaxed enough to take in information and brave enough to do something new. This is when you share together an experience or a discovery. Your kids are watching, so share your learning with your kids! They see you struggle, learn, and grow. As you share your process, your kids develop a deep love of learning, as well as a deep appreciation and respect for you!

Here is some language of play around learning:

"Today, I learned ___ . Cool, huh!?" (curiosity)

"I heard the word "invigorated." Let's think of a time you felt in-vigorated!" (vocab building)

I want to try this new thing / go to this new place... and I need to learn ___ . (adventure & courage)

Communicating in this frame of mind, you make it easier for kids to cope with the stressful situations brought on by divorce and it doesn't stop there. This skill continues through life.

Resilient with Strong Social Connections

Kids and adults with good emotional regulation also seek social support when they need it. They do not bottle up emotions, nor do they expect to "go it alone." They do not avoid situations that are uncomfortable. They believe that there is good on the other side of every situation. They believe that they have people in their court. They know that each situation will pass and that they will ultimately be okay with a sense of stability, love, and security. Using language that leans into play will help you keep the mindset that draws you into joy. This is the healthy other side of divorce for everyone!

The Healthy Other Side of Divorce for my Kids and Me:

I started loving being a single mom. Yes, it was hard work, but I loved not having to negotiate daily schedules, what bedtime was going to look like, the many ways to do a consequence or agreeing about the right way. I loved being able to be in charge of the money. Even though I had significantly less money, I felt like it was more because I could decide where it was going. Embracing a Play Mindset, I began to dream again! I managed to carry out a few key dreams that were transformational! One of those dreams was that I wanted my children to see themselves as World-Citizens, not just as "my-town" citizens. I wanted them to think globally. My first step was to host foreign exchange students: new languages, map studies, cultural exposure, etc. I felt so successful as this formative experience shaped how they see the world. This would not have been possible if I had stayed married. Next, I wanted to travel with them to Europe and visit the University I attended and meet my friends. This trip unfolded in the most unexpected way, and voila! We found ourselves in Europe for 6 weeks with backpacks on our backs! A dream come true.

Even now, Years after divorce, I want my kids
to Believe in their own dreams

I figured there is no better way to instill belief than for me to step into my dream. I dreamed of having my own business. After exploring many options and doing a lot of self-discovery, I birthed *The Language Of Play*. This business is the outcome of my personal experiences married to my skills as a 30-year Speech Language Pathologist. I know how to help parents become the parents they want to be! And, I can teach kids to communicate! Now, I help parents do both!!

Becoming Brave

First, I helped parents by creating a podcast called "The Language Of Play." Clearly parents are yearning for information on how to effectively make change in their homes, because it's a Top 1.5% podcast! Next, I started coaching parents who want to help their children communicate better (with or without a speech delay). Giving back from the experiences in my own life and from my expertise feels natural. I am very proud of the parents I work with for making the amazing transformations in their homes that they seek! My example of diligence and being brave has been good for my now-adult kids. I have needed kind language toward myself during the hard parts, and my kids use the language of play to encourage me.

At the time, I thought that the dissolution of my marriage would crush us. But the pressure cooker of divorce did not crush my kids nor me. It had the power to propel us toward deep healing. In that desperation, we dug down, found support and anchored into our relationship as a complete family. We learned to have a Play Mindset and use the language of play in our conversations so that trust was built.

We apologized often.

We forgave each other often.

We built back trust.

We learned together.

We became resilient.

Our emotions became more regulated.

We learned more and played more.

We began to dream again and dreamed together.

Then, we created together.

And then… they saw me create "The Language Of Play."

We had a new, wonderful, and different life than I expected, and it was good! It still is good!

It is very good.

Dinalynn Rosenbush

Dinalynn Rosenbush is a Consultant and Parenting Coach, Speaker, 30-year school Speech Language Pathologist, international best-selling Author, and Creator/Host of the Top 1.5% podcast: The Language of Play.

Dinalynn helps parents become the parent they want to be, even in the presence of a speech delay. She understands how children communicate and empowers parents to connect more deeply with their children so that they can make the changes they want. She empowers parents with practical, daily strategies that work during normal daily activities to improve communication and speech. Dinalynn enjoys the outdoors and resides in Minnesota where she is near her children and grandchildren.

If you are struggling with hope, wondering what to do with your kiddos and how to adjust, whether in the presence of a speech delay or not, contact Dinalynn Rosenbush at <u>hello@thelanguageofplay.com</u> and she will be sure to reply! Don't be shy. Just write.

CHAPTER 6

Destiny and Transformation

Eleanor Haspel-Portner

To Marvin, My Soul Mate and the Love of My Life.
"And now here is my secret, a very simple secret: It is only
with the heart that one can see rightly; what is essential is
invisible to the eye."
~Antoine de Saint-Exupery—The Little Prince

Have you ever looked back at your life and thought or felt you were on the brink of all you worked for? When I ask that question, I hear a resounding "Yes, you're there." How did I get here, and what was the turning point—the big decision that committed me to my path?

Many detours in my life served as tributaries function in a river. They widened my possibilities without disrupting my life. However, the decision to end my first marriage changed my life in a significant way. With it, I committed to my core life mission and deepened my inner harmony, direction, and joy.

Background

My first husband and I met three weeks before he left for medical school in Chicago. We instantly felt a deep connection and were a couple when he left. Our courtship had some red flags, but I thought we would work through them because he seemed open and accommodating to my spiritual interests and goals. After being accepted at the University of Chicago, LH and I married.

Once I began graduate school, I realized I had to take a firm stand on many important issues. I did that when planning our wedding, and the pattern continued. I generally stay in an even energy and work diligently, living by the mantra, "How you do anything is how you do everything." I did that in my first marriage and took on the "perfect wife" role despite being in graduate school, having two children eleven months apart, and maintaining an active social life.

Although LH's emotions challenged me to remain true to myself, we were a happy couple. I discovered who I truly am during our relationship while living happily and thriving. We lived happily because we:

- were good friends

- were good lovers

- had shared goals in education

- had the same sense of compassion for others

- are of equal intelligence

- have two beautiful and brilliant children

- had compatible parenting styles with our young children

- pushed each other to achieve our fullest potential

- enjoyed the entertainment arts of all kinds in Chicago

- rarely felt dissonance in our points of view

To all our friends, we had what seemed to be a perfect life. And yet, I spent the last two and a half years of that marriage deciding about whether or not to get a divorce.

What Went Wrong?

Often, during my first marriage, I noted that my husband and I had different sensibilities and needs, although we generally resolved our differences peacefully. However, as we both approached graduation and LH began to make money, I began to note an erosion of what I valued. I started feeling pulled toward areas of the Mental/Waking World life that were uncomfortable for me.

It became apparent that my core comfort within myself is my Spiritual/Archetypal Core Values. When we met, LH knew I aspired to be a trained Jungian Analyst and also that, since childhood, I sensed that I wanted to live in California. As I struggled to find balance in my life that began manifesting increasing dissonance, I started having dreams of **K**nowing with a **K.** These dreams began to tell me that I had to stay on course and follow my inner core. As I opened to this reality, it became clear that LH and I had left our journey together and that one or the other of us would have to compromise at the core of who we were most aligned within ourselves to continue to love and support each other.

I struggled with which of the Four Worlds—the Mental/Waking, the Spiritual/Archetypal, the Emotional/Angelic, and the Physical/

Biological—would take priority in my life. When LH and I were married for about a year, I **K**new I had to get a Siamese Cat. LH set some goals for me to achieve before he would agree, and when I met the goals quickly, we adopted Noble, my first cat, who lived for 22 years and changed my life.

The first night Noble was with me, he taught me to trust him, and we bonded at an intense soul level. Noble sat on my desk while I studied, guarded my children, and defended me from anyone he felt was not energetically aligned with me. I gained courage and strength within that I had never known to the same degree before. I knew that if Noble loved me so purely, I could trust myself and my sensibilities. Having Noble by my side gave me the courage to live primarily in the Spiritual/Archetypal World because pets primarily live there. They remind us of that energy and part of ourselves when we are with them.

Ending a Marriage and Thriving

When I finally realized that if I did not leave my marriage I would end up compromising many areas in my life that were important and felt aligned with my inner core, I told LH that I wanted a divorce. LH had set a deadline for my answer about moving into a home we had bought in a suburb of Chicago. I knew my decision was of great importance because it was not a comfortable decision. At my core, I knew the move went against everything I valued, so I decided that no matter the difficulties involved, I had to leave the relationship so both LH and I could have the lives we wanted.

The months after the divorce were fraught with deep soul searching and deep resolve that no matter what challenges I faced as a single mother with two young children and no income, I had to risk it all for the future of myself, my children, and LH.

During moments of clarity after my separation from LH, I resolved to get my license as a psychologist and be successful in helping others stay true to themselves. Along the way, I **K**new with a **K** that I needed to scuba dive. I did not at the time know why, but a Voice told me to scuba dive, and I listened. In the middle of the Chicago winter, I took swimming lessons to get certified as a scuba diver. This drive deep within pushed me to spend time in the water swimming. The discipline and routine of swimming daily in Chicago was augmented by my learning and practicing Transcendental Meditation. Meditation and Being in the water bring me stillness and quiet within, without external energy filtering in. While swimming, I am alone with no other energy frequencies except the water and me.

It took all my inner courage during this adjustment time to put myself forth in the Mental/Waking World as a young professional. I read books on self-help like Napoleon Hill's *Think and Grow Rich*, John Allen's *How Man Thinketh*, and Dale Carnegie's *How to Win Friends and Influence People.* As I read, I pushed myself to take chances meeting people; my confidence that I could be a successful woman on my own soared.

At the time I started meditating, I also had what I came to learn was a Kundalini experience. I was asking myself, "Of what am I afraid?" A bright light enveloped me, and I was shown that my fear was the process of remembering all knowledge during death and then forgetting it when reborn. I was also shown how relationships work and what breaks them apart, confirming for me that my divorce was the right action.

As I came out of that experience, I wrote an outline for a book called *Marriage in Trouble: A Time of Decision,* and I sent the outline to a publisher the next day. Within a couple of weeks, a contract came to me in the mail. I wrote the book that was published in 1976.

Writing the book allowed me to begin making sense of what I had just gone through emotionally and allowed me to self-reflect and analyze what my values were and why and how I had made choices as I did.

Becoming Free

Less than a year after my divorce, I opened a private psychology practice in Chicago and, within several months, had a growing practice. To earn money and experience, I became a Sex Therapist and worked with couples at a Hospital Clinic as their Masters and Johnson trained therapist. I enjoyed building my practice, and it grew.

During this time, I expanded my psychic abilities. My memories of seeing auras surfaced. I began learning about consciousness and esoteric studies, including astrology, meditation, Reiki, past life regressions, and extraterrestrial existence. Most importantly, I learned how to manage and control my abilities.

While on my own, I learned to follow the Voice within, which whispers to me about what to do or what I know. I heard that Voice the first time I visited California. As I drove through the Pacific Coast Highway Tunnel and saw the Pacific Ocean and the cliffs of Pacific Palisades, I started crying, and the Voice said: "This is Home." I felt those words so deeply that within a year I left my very successful practice in Chicago. Because I trusted my **K**nowing, and I believed in myself, I relocated to Pacific Palisades, California.

In Pacific Palisades I began to build a new practice. To succeed, I commuted to Chicago every six weeks for 18 months and did once-a-month therapy with my clients and three-day weekend groups. I began the groups in my Chicago apartment and continued them after I moved for ten years. They were life-changing for clients and allowed my creative intelligence to innovate ways of helping clients gain clarity in consciousness so they could resolve emotional issues and live happily.

God's Hand

My life was filled with work, my children, and dating. Several relationships, although meaningful, were not ones for a long-term future. Then, one day, while meditating in May 1978, a Voice told me to go to Bhagwan Shree Ratheesh's Ashram in Poona, India. I barely knew who Bhagwan was and had no genuine interest in his Ashram, but the Voice told me to go, so I planned a trip. I arranged my work schedule and arranged for my children to be with their Father for the summer.

Sitting in the Indian Taxi with three Indian men on a three-hour journey, I wondered about my sanity as a lone woman in India. I arrived at the Ashram in Poona on July 31, 1978; I was lonely and scared but remembered the song I listened to repeatedly as a child, "Whenever I feel afraid, I whistle a happy tune, and no one ever knows I'm afraid."

I arrived at the Ashram, a fantastic property with gardens and meditation areas everywhere you looked. But I was alone and had no idea where to go or what to expect. I knew very little about Bhagwan and less about the Ashram. I stood frozen and waiting to Know. After finding a rock to sit on, I meditated and waited. After some time, I found myself walking to the office and scheduling to take Sanyas. Sanyas means to become a disciple of the Master. I have always believed that it is best to experience something, as long as it is not permanent, and to judge its value.

When I took Sanyas on August 4, 1978, I felt seen and known by Bhagwan to the depth of my being. The experience of his energy and the movement of energy when he touched my head and looked into my eyes was of being in the void of time and space and knowing the bliss of light energy with no boundaries. As I left the building and walked into the night, I heard the words, "I will never be afraid of the dark again because in the dark is the light of consciousness, and I am it." The energy coursing through me kept me up all night and awakened a new inner depth.

I put my Mental/Waking Self aside and moved with no mind from the core of my being. I began to know at a new level of **K**nowing that being at peace and joy internally was far more meaningful than anyone outside of me thought. I felt alone but with a different sense of what alone was. It was a Self-security that I was a complete and divine being whole within myself and that what I felt and knew about myself was valid for me and gave me meaning for myself. I knew I could share my self-perceptions with others and could even be intimate in a relationship. Still, I knew I could only be in relationships that did not judge or ask each other to compromise themselves.

The Destiny of Souls

The morning, after I grounded myself securely in my self-identity, Majida (Marvin) approached me at one of Bhagwan's recorded lectures and asked me if he could share my blanket. I welcomed him, and we met at the canteen after the lecture. Majida was looking for a friend with a warm shower, so I offered him my hotel shower as an option. (We were in Poona, India, and it was a very informal and openly welcoming community.) We felt a compelling attraction within about half an hour of being in the same proximity. When we were in each other's auras, it felt like we were one being. Neither Majida nor I had ever experienced that kind of oneness.

Majida had left his medical practice in Pacific Palisades, California, because he did not want to practice herd medicine and was not planning to return to the U.S. (We lived within a mile of each other in Pacific Palisades and knew all the same people.) Meanwhile, I was going home to my practice and my children. I decided that first night to allow my relationship with Majida to be whatever it would be. I wanted us each to do what suited us within our individual destinies. If that were aligned, it would be shown to me; if it were not, I would also be okay with it.

Majida told me he did not want to remarry after his traumatic divorce, and he loved being in India, living a life with no schedule or responsibilities except to his internal Self. I understood and supported his process as he supported mine. We spent three weeks together at the Ashram and then traveled to Mumbai before my trip home to California. As we parted at the airport in Mumbai, I told Majida, "Do what is right for you and know that I love you and will be fine with whatever is right for you. Make your decisions about your future based on your inner Voice."

(Majida and I met at the date and time my
mentor astrologer predicted several years earlier.)

Two weeks after I returned to Pacific Palisades, Majida called from the airport and asked to come to my home. My children and I welcomed him, and within two days, he recognized Noble as a healer and bonded securely with him. Majida moved into my home, and we became a family. Majida's family situation challenged our commitment to each other and, more importantly, our Spirituality. We had verbally agreed in our relationship that if one of us was uncomfortable with a decision, we would not proceed. We have followed this agreement for the 46 years we have been together.

After eight months of living together, we bought a home in Pacific Palisades and married. Our life focused on the children and our work. Majida joined my ongoing therapy groups and traveled with me to

Chicago. He slowly restarted his medical practice, spending time with each patient so he could practice medicine as a true healer.

Throughout our marriage, we have remained true to our core values. We meditate and pray first thing every day. We respect each other's space and support each other's self-care. When possible, we do things together.

Several years ago, I was at a family event and looked at LH and his wife. I felt a wave of inner gratitude that I had severed that marriage so that both LH and I could find our soul mates and be happy. As I looked around the room at the people at the family celebration, I recognized the integrity of knowing that comes from the Soul. My choices that had been so agonizingly difficult during my marriage to LH had freed me to find my very Core Self, and I confirmed at that event that I had made the right choices. My choices freed me from living in compromise and freed LH and our children.

I am deeply grateful that the Divine orchestrated abundance and alignment within me and that I listened to the Inner Voice. I dared to leap into the void of the unknown, where I found who I am and how to be in the world.

I encourage everyone to stay true to their inner Self, ask for clarity, and listen for the answers. We are all Divine beings living in a physical body. The more we remain aligned with our Divine mission and live in harmony with who we are as a Spiritual Being, the more joy and inner peace we find and spread to others.

Dr. Eleanor Haspel-Portner

Dr. Eleanor Haspel-Portner passionately synthesizes areas of esoteric wisdom and scientific discovery. Her Ph.D. from the University of Chicago gives her a unique integrative background and perspective.

She has published numerous bestselling books and helped thousands of individuals, couples, and groups practically synthesize life experiences for healthy, prosperous, and creative lives. Dr. Eleanor uses her psychic abilities to delve deeply into all aspects of living. She believes that when you spiritually awaken, radiating love from the core of your being, you live a well-balanced, happy life.

Dr. Eleanor empowers and tunes into the soul of her clients. She is working on an innovative personality theory recognizing that we live in Four Worlds and that living a fulfilling life involves integrating these Worlds. In her work with Noble Energy Wellness, she shows you how to manifest your highest potential to live a life you love. She and her husband, Dr. Marvin, host a weekly free webinar on manifesting your dream life.

Connect with Eleanor at www.nobleenergywellness.com.

CHAPTER 7
My Journey to Peace

Gina Nalbone Phillips

---

*To my parents, Bill and Dolores, who have always
encouraged me to follow my dreams; to my sister, Robyn,
for her unwavering support and cherished friendship; and
to my son, Jason, who is my greatest gift.*

As I sat in the audience of my son's 4th grade graduation, the tears started streaming down my face as the children sang "It's a Wonderful World" by Louis Armstrong. To the outside world it looked as though I had a Wonderful World. I was a stay-at-home mom, my husband was very successful, and we had just built a beautiful new home. We had nice cars, clothes, jewelry and went on fancy vacations. Little did everyone know that we had been in marriage counseling for nine months and I was really trying everything to hold on to our marriage and our family.

In reality, my world was not so wonderful. My plans for myself and my family's future were about to change. The man that I had spent 21 years with no longer wanted the same things that I did. Finally, in August of 2008, only two months after my son's graduation, I asked my husband to move out of the house as it was no longer healthy for us to continue to live a lie in front of our son. I found out not only was he cheating on me with another person, but was also secretly hiding money.

My son started middle school as I started navigating the divorce process and I was scared and confused. What to do next? I had been married for 13 years and had spent the last eight years as a stay-at-home mom. Much of my focus had been meeting the needs of my husband and my son. I really did not know who Gina was. Several things happened during the three years it took for my divorce to finalize: I filed for divorce, a few weeks after that the stock market crash of 2008 happened, the value of our new home dropped 20%, my husband's income dropped 50%, and our investment accounts dropped 20%. These numbers were scary! I had to find better ways to control my finances and all the emotions of a failed marriage. My journey to discover myself and my happiness was not something that happened overnight. It has taken me years and many steps along the way. I have narrowed it down to 13 steps I did to get over my 13-year marriage and I share them below.

STEP 1: Find a Good Therapist

One of the first things I did was find my own therapist. My mind was always working in overdrive, so I needed help processing my thoughts to ensure I was making informed decisions while dealing with all the stress associated with the divorce process. My therapist helped me let go of the guilt I felt regarding my failed marriage and taught me how to process my feelings. I remember her asking me what was something that brought joy to my life? What made Gina happy and wanting to get out of bed each day? How did Gina want to process the divorce and make all the choices that needed to be made throughout the process? I realized that for most of my life I was always worried about what my family and friends thought of me. I was always saying I was sorry for things that really were not my fault. While in therapy, I let go of some of my limiting beliefs and learned that my feelings mattered and it was okay to feel sad or anxious. The next step was to find things that released those feelings and brought joy into my life.

STEP 2: Exercise

Right before turning 40, I decided that I wanted to get healthy and lose some weight. By September 2008, I was already two years into my journey of attending an elite gym. I had a personal trainer three times a week and was following a meal plan to reduce my body fat. I was working hard to look and feel good. Doing cardio and weights really helped build my body and my mind; it helped reduce stress and I realized the importance of exercise in my daily routine. Over the years, I have done many different diets and exercise activities to maintain a healthy lifestyle and found that the endorphins that are released when I exercise really have helped me overcome stress and anxiety.

STEP 3: Knowing My Numbers

During our marriage, I was in charge of our monthly expenses and once I became a stay-at-home mom and my salary was not in the picture I had to budget carefully as the majority of my husband's income was commission. I had a clear picture of our expenses and was able to plan accordingly to pay all of our bills. After he moved out of the house, we had the added expense of maintaining two households. It was also important to track our spending as we started the divorce process. In New York State, our financial statement of net worth is 23 pages long! I found completing that form to be overwhelming even though I have an accounting degree. As I reviewed all my expenses, I developed a clear picture of what I needed to support myself and my son not only now but for my future as a single mother. Knowing my numbers was a big step for me to feel in control of my future. I joke with some of my friends that balancing my checkbook provides me with peace of mind knowing that I can pay all my bills.

STEP 4: Meeting My Tribe

Sharing custody with your ex-spouse is one of the hardest things to do. I knew sitting at home alone drinking a glass of wine was not a good solution to get over my loneliness. I was truly fortunate to find two other mothers who were in the same circumstance with boys the same age. We first started going out to share a meal together and then we started looking for other fun things to do. We soon discovered that we all shared a love of live music and dancing. Each weekend we would find the best places to listen to music and we started meeting other people that were also single after a divorce. Thank God for modern technology, it was easy for us to be added to the text thread to know where and when we would go to enjoy live music together. It was both men and women and we ranged in age from earlier 40s to late 50s and there was a sense that we had known each other for years. We soon started gathering at each other's homes for parties and celebrations and I soon volunteered to host the Superbowl. I have been hosting this annual party for 12 years now and I am officially known as "Superbowl Gina." To this day, I am happy to still call these people my friends!

STEP 5: Getting a Dog

Having an animal to give you unconditional love is one the best feelings in the world. My husband was allergic so we could not have a dog.

We had not officially told our son of our plans to divorce. One Sunday night after getting back from his dad's apartment, my son approached me and said, "Look on the bright side. If you and daddy get a divorce, we can get a puppy." Even at ten years old he was trying very hard to look on the bright side of a bad situation. A few months later for my birthday we went down to the SPCA to look for a dog and we walked through the whole shelter, but no puppies were there. We turned the corner and there was a 4-month-old German Shephard mix breed, his paws three times the size of his body. We brought him into the meet and greet room and boy did that dog know it was time to be on his best behavior. He was playing so gently with my son and even allowed us to rub his belly. I was still unsure and told my son, "Look at those paws. H's going to be very big." This puppy then licked my face and put his head on my lap and that was it, I knew that we had found our dog! Mickey was the best dog ever. He was a gentle giant weighing in at 100 pounds and loved his belly rubs. Mickey gave me such purpose every weekend that my son was not there. I knew I was never alone.

STEP 6: My Faith

Ever since I was a little girl, I have always had a strong sense of faith and found prayer centering for me. I am Catholic and enjoy attending mass every week and as Friday approaches I am always figuring out which mass will fit in with my weekend activities. My Catholic education has been the one constant in my life. I attended Catholic school from kindergarten through college graduation. As I sat in church one Sunday in the middle of March of 2011, I saw an ad for a part-time bookkeeper working 24 hours per week at my Church. I remember my son looking over my shoulder telling me that would be a perfect job for me. After over nine years of being a stay-at-home mother, I updated my resume and applied for the job. I had a lot of fear about working outside the home again and I think a combination of being an active member of the church, my accounting degree, and having over 15 years of experience helped me get the job. This was a major step in me moving on from my previous life.

STEP 7: Reading and Setting Up a Routine

I have always had a love of reading. But once I became a wife and a mother, I never could find the time to read. It was important to rediscover the things that brought joy into my life. I am old school when it comes to reading as I enjoy going to a bookstore and holding a book in my hands to determine if it's calling to me to learn more. I also love to have an inspirational bookmark to keep my place and after I discovered self-help books, my world felt full of possibilities. Over the years I have read some amazing books to guide me on my new path. The subject matter that has helped me the most was a book about setting up a routine to start your day.

Here is my morning routine: I start my day listening to a 5-minute meditation and opening up all the blinds to let the sunshine in as my cup of coffee is brewing. Next, I feed my dog and as he eats his breakfast, I make my bed and then take the dog for a short walk to breathe in the fresh air as I listen to a recording of me speaking the current goals I have set for all aspects of my life. Back in the house, I say my 24 positive affirmations in the mirror, a few prayers, and then I write in my journal. This gets my mind focused and started for the day.

STEP 8: The Woo Woo Stuff

So, what do I mean about the "woo woo" stuff? One of the first things I did after my husband moved out was have a psychic reading. There were things that she knew about me and my situation that were very surprising and life changing. I was ready to figure out what was important to me and how to move on from my fears. Around the same time, a friend of mine took a Reiki class and wanted to practice on me. Reiki is a form of energy healing that helps you release blocked energy from the seven chakras in your body. It made a lot of sense to me when she told me that my throat chakra was blocked, because most of my life I did not speak my truth. Over the years, I have attended a full range of "woo woo" activities including full and new moon ceremonies, sound healings and reiki circles, and had various energy clearings performed on me. During the pandemic, I discovered feng shui and attended an online class. Feng shui is an ancient Chinese geomancy that harnesses energy forces between an individual and their environment. I hired a feng shui professional to align my living and office space. The simple act of rearranging a desk or bed can help the energy flow freely. I also have tapped into my own intuition and gut feelings about people and places. All these things have helped me realize that there is a great big world out there full of possibilities.

STEP 9: Buying My Own House

As my son was starting his senior year of high school, I realized that I no longer wanted or needed to live in the house I built with my ex-husband. It had been about four years since the divorce was finalized and what was I going to do with a 3,000-square foot house while my son was off to college? And, how was I going to afford all the costs associated with maintaining the property? For the first time in my life, I could pick where I wanted to live and not worry about the school district or what anyone else wanted. I wanted to be able to walk to stores and restaurants yet still be close to nature. When I walked into my current house, I was able to look past all the work that needed to be done and envision what I wanted for my living space. I can walk to wonderful amenities and am a block away from a park and waterfall. The new home is a two-family home and allows my 18-year-old son and I to each have our own living space.

STEP 10: Finding My Purpose

I recall the summer before my son went away to college and I realized I still was not completely happy. A good friend of mine who was a financial planner told me about a certification that helps people with their finances during the divorce process called a Certified Divorce Financial Advisor. He said with your personal and professional experience this would be a perfect job for you. A few months later, five months before my 50th birthday, I left my job and started studying to obtain my certification.

In July 2017, I officially started my own business, WNY Divorce Financial Advisors, LLC. The vision for my business really started back in 2009 in the middle of my divorce, and the more time I spent with my friends in similar circumstances, the more I realized there had to be a better way. I talked about starting some type of business to help with the whole divorce process as it should not take years to complete. The lawyers know the law regarding divorce but the CDFAs of the world know the numbers. Everyone needs a clear picture of their numbers. It provides a sense of security for a future after the divorce, and I know that with proper planning and realistic goals you can be in control of your own financial stability.

STEP 11: Hiring a Coach

Soon after I started my business, I realized that I could not do it alone and hired my first business coach back in 2018. Since that time, I have had several different types of coaches both personal and professional. Coaches are always pushing you past your fears and helping you reframe your mindset. They guide you but coaching only works if you do the homework they give you. I know that I will always have some type of coach helping me to continue to evolve in my personal, professional and spiritual growth. It's never too late to learn new technology, or just a new way of looking at things. One of the biggest lessons I've learned is not everyone is going to like you or respect your decisions but you can choose how you react.

STEP 12: Self-Care

I have learned over the years the importance of self-care. Most of my life I was a people-pleaser and not addressing my own needs. Therefore, everyday my first affirmation as I look in the mirror is, "I must love myself first"! That is a very powerful statement. To love yourself you must do things that make you happy and bring joy into your life. Over the years, my self-care rituals have changed. Yes, getting a massage and my nails done is a form of self-care, but for me it is also walking in nature smelling the fresh air and exploring new places. It's spending time with my friends, dancing to music or just enjoying a conversation, and other times it is me staying home with my current 80-pound rescue dog watching a movie. When you learn how to maintain your own self-care, you can spread all your light into the world.

STEP 13: Practicing Gratitude

Christmas 2019 I received a gratitude journal as a gift and on Jan 1, 2020, I started writing in the journal every night before I went to bed. At first it was hard to think of things to write down every day but once the pandemic hit in March 2020 and my son was sent home from college, like many of us my whole world changed. Taking a moment every night to reflect on things I was grateful for changed my perspective. Sometimes it is the simple things like seeing a bluejay in the middle of winter or catching up with a friend for dinner. I think the thing I am most grateful for is my divorce. I am grateful for all the time I was able to spend with my son making memories. I am grateful for my family and tribe because of their unconditional love and support. I am grateful for my journey over the last 13 years that has helped me find myself and my purpose. I am grateful for my clients because each time I help them I guide them on a journey to their financial stability and getting to the other side of divorce.

Establishing a routine as created freedom and peace in my life. If you don't have a routine, I highly recommend stating with just one thing and then adding on to it as you master that one thing.

As Les Brown says, "You don't have to be great to start, but you have to start to be great!"

Are you ready to find peace in your life? Why wait?

Gina Phillips

Gina Phillips is the owner of WNY Divorce Financial Advisors, LLC, where she passionately dedicates herself to empowering individuals navigating marital transitions to regain control over their financial well-being. As a skilled liaison between clients and divorce mediators and attorneys, Gina is driven by personal experience and a deep understanding of the challenges that accompany divorce. Her pursuit of certification as a Divorce Financial Analyst (CDFA®) demonstrates her commitment to providing comprehensive support.

With over 30 years of experience in auditing and accounting fields, Gina brings a wealth of knowledge to her practice. Her certification as a CDFA® combined with her expertise enables her to offer compassionate and cost-effective assistance. Whether you are in the early stages of considering a divorce or currently navigating the complexities of the legal proceedings, Gina will guide you with empathy and expertise to ensure your transition is as smooth and financially secure as possible.

Connect with Gina at https://www.wnydivorcefinancial.com/contact.php.

CHAPTER 8

Seven Golden Nuggets to Thrive After Divorce

Gwen Lepard

To all those who've suffered verbal abuse, may your life become what you truly desire.

To all who've given up on doing what they love… Commit to doing it! The way will reveal itself.

To anyone who's afraid to dance but really wants to, please… DANCE!

It's late 2011, and I'm on a dinner cruise off the coast of Orange County, California. I'm with a group of Next Level speakers, authors, entrepreneurs, and other super cool individuals. The person who introduced me to this group had dubbed me "The Joy Authority" and I danced with joy, talked about joy, and shared how to have joy yourself.

What I hadn't done yet was share my story.

It was my turn at the mic and I said, "On July 31, 2009, after years of verbally whipping me, my husband finally did it for real. That day, I fled my Montana home and began my journey back to me." It was the first time I'd shared that part of my journey.

Afterward, a speaker and NLP trainer from the group told me he could now believe my joy. Having heard my experience of pain and suffering, he said, "Now your joy makes sense." Before when all I shared was joy, joy, joy it didn't ring true to him.

Thank you so much for being here and reading my story. In this chapter, I'll share life stories and Seven Golden Nuggets I learned after my divorce. These nuggets help me live an ever-evolving life with a core of joy. I'm grateful for my journey… All of it.

Golden Nugget 1: It's Okay to Share Your Pain and Struggles

Let's get back to the rest of the above story. He, my husband at the time, whipped me with a pair of wet pants. The zipper came around and hit me in the corner of my left eye. I still remember the sting. This was after he'd thrown coffee on me in front of the washer and dryer. As I was trying to clean up the mess, he used those pants as a whip. Then he screamed at me, "I'm going to keep coming down on you harder and Harder until you stop doing Stupid stuff." The stupid thing that I did… was my job, the laundry.

Maybe you already know this, but the truth is, as humans we connect through stories of pain and suffering. Sure, we love to hear stories of success, but we can better believe them when that success comes through a trial by fire.

Social media is a great example. Put up a post about a success and sure some will comment and cheer you on, but put up a picture in the ER or share an illness, loss, or trouble and so many will flock to give advice, comfort, and want to help. It's part of human nature.

Asking for help by being vulnerable about what's happening in your world can open doors that may surprise you when you're in it. I've also found that, especially when you're beyond those struggles, the reality of what you experienced connects and shows you as someone others can relate to and want to follow.

So share your struggles, pains, and challenges. It helps you and others.

Golden Nugget 2: Knowledge Is Power - Awareness Is the First Step in Healing

My former husband was a narcissist. I didn't want to believe it and I didn't completely until 10 years after the fateful day that he whipped me for real.

It was when a friend offered to introduce me to a telesummit leader saying, "You're really good at what you do, you're just not talking to the right people."

She shared that I'd need a niche. Niching is essential for telesummit success and she suggested helping those who'd been affected by narcissists as she knew some of my story.

Let me share a bit more. A few years after leaving my husband, I got involved in a business partnership with an even more extreme personality. During that time, I met a guy who I became deeply involved with who turned out to be a covert narcissist. It was so subtle, the love bombing felt good after having had two verbally abusive relationships, and I didn't know what to look for at the time. I was unaware that if the frequency that attracts energy bullies is still in your energy field, you'll keep finding those types showing up in your life.

As I explored that niching idea, gaslighting came up, a form of psychological abuse. It uses a combination of brainwashing, psychological bullying, and emotional abuse to control and dominate. It was through a psychcentral.com article, "7 Gaslighting Phrases Malignant Narcissists, Sociopaths, and Psychopaths Use to Silence You," that I finally fully accepted that my former husband was a narcissist.

That knowledge led me to create over a dozen programs and courses containing knowledge, energy clearings, and many meditations to empower empaths, like myself, who are the favorite "food" of those personality types.

I'm not an expert on personally types; however, I am an expert in bringing awareness and creating energy tools to regain your power so that healing can begin. Awareness is the first step in the 5-step process of healing. The tools I've created help support, empower, and strengthen sensitive individuals so they can be stable, secure, and strong, which repels the energy bully types.

Remember, the knowledge of what you're dealing with or have dealt with gives you power over it. You can stop unconsciously feeding those personality types by becoming aware, beginning the healing, and taking your power back.

Golden Nugget 3: Invest in Yourself and Commit Completely

Let's backtrack to the verge of another defining pivot point that led to the revealing mic moment on the boat. It was January 2011 and I was soon to become a seminar junky.

It all began with a women, wine, and networking event. The venue was a cozy wine bar in Mission Valley, San Diego (I still drank at the time). There we were surrounded by warm dark wooden walls and having great conversations, sipping chardonnay, and enjoying the charcuterie board when a young man got up to talk. He was our speaker for the evening. I don't remember what he said and I didn't know what he had, but I wanted it!

He gave away a DVD program and I won it. He made an offer and I said yes. I signed up for a weekend workshop. Still, I had no idea what I signed up for; I was going totally on instinct. Turns out it was Neuro-Linguistic Programming (NLP), Hypnosis, Coaching, Leadership training, and more… There was so much that I learned, so many shifts and changes just during that weekend. I was hooked.

There was an offer to go further. At that time in my life, I would never have signed up for something like the programs they were talking about.

But these were "certification programs" you learned so you could help others and get paid for it. I wouldn't do it for me, but I could for others. Of course, the beauty of that is that I received a lot of the healing that I needed through the training.

As it turns out, I took almost every program and course they offered, crewed for events, and ended up working in the back office of the company. I committed completely to the process I invested in. It removed all the mental fog and emotional numbness that had resulted from the years of verbal abuse. It completely changed my life. I got my joy back.

I attended many different seminars by different leaders on different topics. It was exciting, so many wonderful people to meet, so much connection, and there was always music during the breaks. So… I danced! I believe it was the fact that I was so engaged in the presentations and that I danced during the breaks (even if no one else was) that got me the "Joy Authority" title.

During that time, I met a remarkable energy healer and spent two years with her, learning the science of energy work. Even when traveling to Australia, Fiji, Canada, and Hawaii, I showed up for all but two of the calls. Her approach to the body that leads to wellness included clearing relationship residue, which was of great help when I started creating courses of my own.

I learned about the different styles of leadership. The thing that most aligned with me was the Guide by the Side style. Learning that I didn't have to have it all together, that I could still be dealing with having been a victim, with being a people pleaser, with years of verbal abuse, and still being able to help others was incredibly eye-opening!

So I committed to putting together a talk on Joy and creating offers to share during an event. I got some clients. I was doing the work, making a difference, and I loved helping get clients out of anxiety and into a more joyful life.

When you say yes to investing in yourself, changes begin right away. Your subconscious is already creating new pathways, and when you commit to giving it your best, who knows what life-altering results you'll experience.

Golden Nugget 4: Sticks and Stones May Break Your Bones, But Words Can Scar You Deeply and to Your Core

The scars caused by words can rob you of your identity, self-esteem, and ability to move forward in life. Read on to see where I'm going with this.

Going to so many seminars and events, I met people who offered many opportunities. One was an online radio show.

Back in the day, I was a radio personality. Getting offered an online radio show of my own seemed like a dream come true. In all my previous gigs, I'd only moved music and information. Getting to decide on the content was joyful. I was a Chief Joy Officer and Joy Authority, so I named the show "Joyful Living Radio."

Even though I had a platform, and I knew there needed to be more awareness about verbal abuse, those scars hadn't yet healed enough for those more challenging conversations. I just wanted to talk about joy, interview experts on joy, and bring more joy into the world.

All the same, there needs to be more awareness of verbal abuse. That it IS abuse and while you don't see the evidence of it on the skin in bruises or broken bones, it scars. The scars can be deep and may take many years to heal. It shows up in a lack of self-esteem, the constant need to apologize, chronic pain, anxiety, and depression. Over time, it can also cause abnormalities in your brain.

Children may say, "Sticks and stones may break my bones but words can never hurt me," as a taunt back at a bully. However, the truth is, words that belittle, ridicule, assault, degrade, or manipulate another are abuse and they leave scars.

My father said, "At least he's not hitting you," about a former boyfriend. It's that lack of awareness that I pray is brought to an end around verbal abuse. I didn't know I was being abused until a counselor said to me, "What he's doing to you IS abuse!"

That knowledge gave me the power to heal those hidden wounds. Perhaps you've experienced verbal, emotional, or psychological abuse. I want you to remember that it is abuse, and you deserve support, healing, and to live a spectacular life beyond what happened.

Golden Nugget 5: You Can Choose How You Respond

Fast forwarding to when a healer client was concerned about the news coming out around the events of 2020 and asked me what to do, I said, "Raise your vibration," and then created a 7-week course to help her, myself, and others raise their frequency and release the pervasive fear, uncertainty, and doubt of the time.

Raising your frequency to joy and above is one of the best things you can do for your health and well-being. It's very helpful to do when you're at a loss over what to do in a situation or you have something that bothers you and you have no control over it.

How do you raise your frequency? There are many ways, and I want to share a favorite with you.

I'd like to offer you the "Easy Breath." You breathe without thought to stay alive, yet you can raise your frequency and transform your life when you bring consciousness to your breath.

Your body knows how to take an "Easy Breath." The diaphragm (the dome-shaped muscle of respiration located at the bottom of your ribs) expands, and air rushes in. Then it contracts back up, and air rushes out.

The simple act of being aware of your breathing is a vibration-raising exercise. Doing three breaths in a row can relax you, help you find answers to questions, and release endorphins to help you feel good.

There are so many things to deal with in life, and wherever you are on your journey, having a tool that helps you respond instead of react raises your frequency. It's a valuable tool allowing you to attract more of what you want.

Golden Nugget 6: Step Out of Your Comfort Zone

Since my divorce, I've stepped out of my comfort zone in many ways and in one very impactful way, I was pushed out. Read on for three stories about comfort zones.

In 2012 I became the Chief Joy Officer and personal assistant to a motivational speaker. I learned the business of being a speaker and making offers from the stage. It was something that I wanted to do myself, even though it was a big step out of my comfort zone.

We traveled, met many fascinating people, and made a difference. My position had me looking for what was going right and was joyful.

While that sounded like a cherry gig, old patterns, programming, and human survival wiring came up to show me all that could go wrong. Talk about uncomfortable. I so wanted to stay in my joy zone, and between my subconscious and life, plenty more being out of my comfort zone awaited me.

In March of 2013, I was pushed out of my comfort zone when my dad died. It was heart-wrenching. It didn't need to happen. Somedays I still struggle with his loss even though I've been through all the stages of grief.

Loss is a process. When it's fresh (this can also be said of divorce), it's like you're getting tossed around in the ocean. Then you make your way to where you can touch the ground. You're still in it and you feel a lot, but there are days when you can get a deep breath again.

After a time, you move out of the ocean. Then one day you'll be on the beach and a big wave will get you and you'll feel the loss again as if it were fresh, but you'll recover faster.

Give yourself time to grieve without guilt and down the road, when a random wave shows up, feel what you feel; the grief will flow back out to the ocean.

October of 2013 saw the launching of Joy Centered Life, the company that I still run today after many pivots and times of wondering if I should shut down shop. When I discovered that my company was designed to evolve, like me, to be ever-evolving while centered around joy, I regained purpose while acknowledging that it's okay to ask for help, to transform from your original vision, and to thrive!

The most recent pivot brought to full circle a support group that I'd created to help increase productivity and help sensitive entrepreneurs, writers, and authors get "it" done with fun. Now, I joyfully hold space to complete many "spinning plates" for myself and others while taking time to dance and move our bodies.

Owning a business, the unnecessary loss of a parent, and speaking while making offers from a stage are only three ways I've repeatedly stepped out of my comfort zone. Your steps out of your comfort zone may be very different, and I trust you will find as much growth and magic on the other side of your steps as I have mine.

May you find the inspiration you've been waiting for and step outside your comfort zone. The rewards are worth it.

Golden Nugget 7: Do What You Love

In 2014, I discovered Dance Church, a community that gets the healing, the joy of dance, and how important it is to do it regularly. For the first time, I have women friends who've become close and have stayed in my life.

Movement is medicine and so many of us sit at a computer for hours a day. I often do.

I came out feet first. My mom touching my feet was the first human touch I experienced, and I've danced my entire life.

Dance Church gives me community, purpose, and a place to be myself in my dance.

I dance to move energy, to process information, to bring joy into my body, and to express what I'm feeling at the time. It is the most creative, generative, and rewarding thing that I do.

I know that dancing the way I do isn't for everyone and everyone can dance or at least move their body in a way that feels good to them.

Since August 2022, I've been a member and dancer in a spiritual dance company that welcomes multiple generations, skill levels, and modalities. Even though, at the time I joined, odd health episodes were messing with my ability to function and work, I was able to dance.

Dancing in a more structured environment contributed to my health gradually returning to wellness. My brain became more alive and I have learned choreography.

Doing what you love brings contentment and joy and reflects your life purpose… Being yourself.

Thank you for reading. Whenever this book finds you, may these stories and Seven Golden Nuggets give you jumping-off places, tools, and inspiration to thrive beyond your divorce or life challenges.

Gwen Lepard

As a Purpose Coach and Dancer, Gwen Lepard inspires sensitive entrepreneurs, writers, and authors who struggle with getting important work done to combine purposeful, focused action with movement to accomplish those difficult-to-get-done business tasks with fun and in much less time than if attempted alone.

She connects sensitive entrepreneurs to their purpose and helps clear the patterns, programs, and projections keeping them seeking, angsting, and second-guessing, while secretly feeling worthless so that they can BE themselves and Love who they BE.

She's a Speaker, an International Bestselling Award-Winning Author, and a Mentor. She has an entire toolshed of healing modalities, including Energy Medicine, Hypnotherapy, NLP, Quantum Jumping, and an Ancient Healing Soul Language.

When you work with Gwen, she's like a guide by the side bringing powerful resources to help you remove the energetic shackles that keep you from living the life you dream of and being who you're meant to be.

When not connecting people with their purpose, you can find her dancing with joy, taking nature walks, doing Block Therapy, curling up with a book, movie, or a tiny home video, or creating healthy whole foods and treats. She's passionate about creating radiant relationships that stand the test of time.

And her joy is seeing you love living your purpose and increasing your vitality, clarity, and energy.

Connect with Gwen at https://gwenlepard.com.

CHAPTER 9

It's Never Too Late to Reinvent Yourself

Jasmina Egelnor

This story is dedicated to my beautiful kids. They are my sunshine, my deepest love and my legacy. To Adam and Isak, I love you beyond lifetimes.

When I got married at 26 years old, I didn't imagine that I would be living my life as a single mom.

I met my ex-husband when I was 19. I was very young, didn't really know who I was, and didn't have much chance to explore who I was and to express my true self during my upbringing.

I was raised to be and behave in a certain way, and there was not much interest from my parents in my true personality, my dreams and wants. It left me feeling less worthy than others. I understand this now, but didn't for many years, not even in my early adulthood. This feeling of unworthiness expressed itself by me putting everybody else before me, always taking care of others, making sure that everybody else's needs were met before mine. I didn't have any personal boundaries and said yes to everyone and everything. And when I said no, I felt such quilt. There was awareness at some level that I was worthy of more, but I kept suppressing that. I kept holding myself back.

All of this created suppressed emotions, frustration and sadness within me. For many years, I was living like this. In my personal and business life. With my loved ones, my colleges and my friends.

So, when I met my ex-husband, I was desiring connection, love, friendship. We became best friends and experienced a lot of good times together. He was and is a lovely man, with a good heart and a bright mind. We share many values and interests. We spent 10 years together before we had kids and had a lot of time to travel together and share a life. It was a good life, filled with care, friendship, love, and experiences.

I was content with my life, but I always had a feeling that something was missing. It was like a black hole that, no matter how hard I tried to fill it, stayed empty. I guess I knew deep inside that life could be more, that I could be more. I wanted to feel happy, fulfilled. I knew that I was settling in life, not using my full potential but I didn't know how to get out of that.

On top of that, I was stuck in my old behavior of pleasing my parents and taking care of everybody else before myself, including my husband to the point that he (and I) never even knew the true me. It wasn't because I was hiding me, but because I was stretching myself so much to meet his needs and to be in his box, that he never had the chance to understand my identity. He didn't see or understand all I was giving up (myself) to please him. I had always done that, and he was used to it. It left me feeling more and more taken for granted and unappreciated. It wasn't his fault; I never stood up for myself. I had no personal boundaries. And it cost me a lot. With time, feelings of frustration, feeling stuck and unloved entered my heart, stronger and stronger.

After I graduated with my master's at the university, life was hectic. Work required a lot, and I was very ambitious and driven to climb the corporate ladder. I never loved my job nor the corporate world, but that was the only way I knew to accomplish things and have success. And that was also what was expected from me since childhood. So, I just kept running and achieving level after level, thinking that someday I would finally find that job, or title, or something that would make me feel fulfilled. I was trying to fill that black hole with success and accomplishments, but it wasn't what I needed or wanted. I wanted to feel joy, purpose, deep love, satisfaction, excitement for life. I would later discover that I was doing it all wrong.

How little I knew back then. I wasn't connected to my heart. I believe I was scared to look deep inside, and to find out how far I was from who I really was and what I desired. So, I kept living from my mind, the safe place. I didn't really know myself at all. And I suppressed her for so many years to make everybody else happy instead.

One thing, though, I could never suppress was my desire for change, to experience more, to expect more of life. Despite all the limiting beliefs put on me, I had big dreams. I have always had a big, colorful imagination and a thirst for more out of life. And I have always had this inner knowing that so much more was possible, a deep faith in possibility and in something greater. That kept me going, no matter what.

Still, there were always opposite emotions in me. Despite deep faith, I tried to suppress my feelings for years and make myself accept being content with my life. I remember telling myself:

"You can't have it all. Maybe you can have success and money, but you will probably never find true purpose, deep love and pure joy. Be grateful for what you have and accept life as it is."

Telling myself these words and the feelings they created in me came from the only truth I knew. I had evidence of success and accomplishment throughout my entire life. That was something that I controlled and something that I was good at. But love, self-love, and just allowing myself to feel joy was something different. My mother had, with her own words, said to me that I should settle when it comes to love and give all of me to success, titles and accomplishment. I believe that she meant well and thought she was protecting me. What she was pushing me to achieve in life was also something she had been wanting for herself but never had. Those weren't my dreams.

I never felt unconditionally loved by my parents; instead, I always felt like I needed to work hard to earn their love, and it left me feeling unworthy. Unworthy of love. Unworthy of enough self-love to put myself first. It took many years to understand this and then a lot of inner work to change it.

And I did change it! Today I feel grateful for everything I have been through. It made me resilient, strong and after understanding and changing my beliefs, I feel powerful from within.

Going back to my marriage, I did experience deep happiness. It arrived with the birth of my two healthy, beautiful boys, only two years apart. Being their mother is a big part of my happiness and purpose in life.

With the birth of our children, life became more intense and stressful. I still pursued my career and took on most of the responsibility in our home and taking care of the kids. I had no time for myself, and I didn't do much for my own joy, except for being with my kids.

My marriage became a teamwork of two people, where my ex-husband performed some activities, and I did the rest. We had our jobs, took care of the kids, planned our daily life, but we had no real marriage, no passion, no deep conversations. We didn't fight but I felt that I was on the edge of losing myself completely. It made me feel sad, angry, and empty.

At this point, I started to dig deeper into myself and understand myself more, bit for bit. I realized I had so many beliefs and stories about myself, that I didn't want to have anymore. I only had those thoughts and feelings, because somebody else told me to believe in those stories and I took them in as mine. The truth is, they never were truly mine.

I realized I was living a lie, a lie about myself. I told myself these lies for so long that I believed them. But they weren't true. I wanted to free myself, to understand my true being, my purpose. I knew there was more of me, more to life.

I also understood how different me and my ex-husband were. Even if we shared friendship and many values, which is important, we were still so different in personalities. I had been stretching myself so much to meet him in his own box, that he probably never noticed our differences. And when my needs to express myself, become more of myself, follow my own wants got stronger, he simply couldn't meet me there. Instead, we fell apart even more. And I got more frustrated, angry and sad, keeping it all inside.

One day, I knew that if we didn't get a divorce, we might end up losing our friendship and the connection we shared as parents. I knew that I couldn't keep it all inside anymore. I felt like I was a ticking bomb. My kids deserved better, and I was worthy of more.

It took me more than three years to finally make the decision to end my marriage.

After the divorce, I experienced a lot of darkness. Nobody knew on the outside, but for months I felt like I had no ground. I had so much guilt about destroying my kids' family, their safety. That's what I told myself. And I was going crazy every time my kids were with their father and away from me. I missed them so much; I could barely handle it. Coming home to an empty apartment felt like my heart was ripped out, repeatedly.

I guess I needed to fall so deeply to rise again like a phoenix rising from the ashes. Deep inside I knew I did the right thing, for me and my kids. I started to look deep inside my heart to understand who I was and what I wanted in life. I needed to learn to be with myself. I needed to learn to love myself. I went deep into personal growth, taking courses, reading books and having coaches. I also tried different business opportunities, looking for something that would give me purpose and joy.

It's been a beautiful journey of awakening, growth, trial and error, rebirth and purpose.

It wasn't easy and there were some challenging days and moments. I kept believing in the light and the knowing that I would find my path. Investing time, energy and money in my personal growth has been the best thing I have ever done for myself. And I will always keep investing in myself.

I didn't know that life could be so different when you embrace your true self and your purpose. It's beautiful.

Me and my ex-husband have a beautiful relationship now. We raise our kids in complete agreement and through deep parental connection. We are best friends and help each other in life. I love him as my family and always will. And I am grateful for the years we spent together and mostly for the two beautiful souls we share, our kids.

We spend Christmas and holidays together as a family. We have even travelled together. We eat dinners together, talk and enjoy seeing our kids grow up. We are very synchronized when it comes to raising our kids and want to create the best possible environment for them to grow up.

My kids are thriving, becoming the best versions of themselves. They are loved and supported by both of their parents.

This is my story and my life and what is possible for me. And I believe it's possible for so many others as well. With that said, I want to point out that it's also completely normal and understandable that not every ex-couple can have the kind of relationship we are privileged to have. It depends on what you have been through, and even more on what both of you are willing to be and do to create a better relationship. I know that it's possible, to have a better relationship, for anyone willing to create one. It does take effort from both people. No matter what your ex-partner is willing to become or do or not, you always have the choice to become the best you can be, for yourself and your kids. You can always become more aware, change, evolve and create a life that you want to live. It's every individual's own decision and choice to make changes and to grow. You can only change yourself.

My self-awareness is very high nowadays, and I am always raising it. I know who I am and who I came here to be.

I left my corporate safety a few years ago and started my own business. I still leverage some of my previous experiences and work as a corporate consultant. And what I truly love doing today is being a life coach and working with other growth-orientated souls, helping them to become their highest selves and live an extraordinary life.

I take good care of myself, have clear personal boundaries and a sense of deep self-love. I feel happy inside, no matter what the outside world looks like. I feel free, at peace and abundant.

My health and wellness are very important to me, and I keep learning and expanding within this field. I love cooking and eating healthy, exercising, practicing mindfulness and self-care. I spend as much time as possible in nature, in sunlight and moving my body. Having a healthy lifestyle brings so much positive energy and well-being to me. This is also something I help my clients with. Everything starts with your health and energy. When we are healthy, we can do anything.

Me and my kids live in a beautiful little house close to nature and the city. I am so grateful for everything I have experienced in life, every single moment. Without it, I wouldn't be here today, I wouldn't be who I am, and I wouldn't have my precious children.

I am enjoying every moment with my kids, as much as possible. I love everyday life, being involved in their life, school, activities and their development. I also enjoy experiencing more expanding and exciting things with my kids, like travelling to different destinations to experience different cultures, food, people, or enjoy activities like skiing. I feel much more present than I did before. There is so much joy when you truly experience the present moment.

I fully understand that a big part for creating a beautiful life for many, especially single parents, is finances. Travelling, experiencing things, activities, anything really costs quite a bit. And being single puts so much more pressure on personal finances. I could go deeper on this, but this is not the time nor the place. All I will say for now is that it's possible to create a stable and even abundant financial status, no matter where you are today. Yes, I have some advantages here, having a long background from corporate finance and good knowledge of personal finances but it hasn't been easy for me still. And I have made some big mistakes when it comes to money and finances, and still I have been able to turn it around every time. It's a lot about mindset and, of course, about knowledge and learning by doing. I know that many people struggle with this, and that's why I help people with their money mindset as well as their financial literacy. Energy (health) and finances are very important vehicles to create the life you desire.

I want to create so much more, for me and my kids. And I am enjoying the journey every day. I am so grateful for the opportunity to share my story with others, and to help many others on their way. It gives me so much joy and fulfilment to see others grow and to keep growing myself.

It's so inspiring and fulfilling to meet like-minded people who are striving for growth and impact too. My new path led me to a whole new world that was unknown to me. My world is so much bigger now, and not limited to my closest environment. I have met so many beautiful souls, learned so much, and have had so many experiences these past few years. The new opportunities, doors opening, new friendships, more abundance and joy and expanded my world.

Joy is inside all of us. We just need to know how to connect to our true self and keep growing. That's when pure joy awakens. It's not the same kind of joy that you feel in short moments of laughing with your kids or your friends. That joy is precious too. But the joy I am telling you about is a different kind. It's a feeling of constant calmer joy, satisfaction, fulfillment and purpose, and gratitude. Keeping a joyful heart, no matter what the outside world looks like. Bouncing back to that joy quickly, even when you fall for a moment. It's simply knowing that you are all you need, all you need is inside of you. Your joy is there, in you, not something that might happen to you. Simply knowing makes you happy.

Life will always go up and down, and it's up to us to make our own interpretations. It's up to us to choose how we feel, how we react and act. Everything is a choice.

I am dedicated to my own growth, to service to others and to keep creating the life I want to live. It's never too late to reinvent yourself and to find your purpose. You can feel joy, fulfillment, peace and abundance, no matter how far you are from feeling that today. It only takes a decision to start, to invest in you, your heart and purpose. And your kids will thrive when your light shines brighter. The whole world will rise its frequency with your own empowerment.

Don't keep diming your light. Take the leap of faith, and step into your own power. Today is the day. Decide.

Jasmina Egelnor

Jasmina Egelnor is a quantum coach, author, and an entrepreneur. Jasmina is dedicated to contributing to raising universal awareness and making a positive impact in the world. Jasmina loves inspiring and coaching people from around the world, to overcome their fears, find their purpose and step into a higher version of themselves, to create and live the life they truly desire.

Jasmina had a long career as a corporate leader before she became an entrepreneur. Despite an amazing career, Jasmina was never passionate about her previous work, except for one area, leadership and coaching. Her experiences and knowledge in business and life, in combination with a deep passion to help other people, led her to another path.

Through her life coaching practice, today Jasmina helps people find their purpose and create freedom in their life. Freedom from inside out, where they can feel free and joyful, no matter their circumstances. Jasmina also coaches people to create their own version of external freedom in terms of place, time and finances.

Jasmina has two teenage sons and lives in Sweden. Besides personal growth and coaching, Jasmina is passionate about health and energy work. Jasmina loves being in nature and experiencing new places and people. Jasmina also enjoys the simple moments in everyday life, like cooking and eating beautiful food, mindfulness and reading. Jasmina's guiding light is love and growth, and that is what she is forwarding further, through her energy and service to others.

Connect with Jasmina on LinkedIn at

https://www.linkedin.com/in/jasmina-egelnor.

CHAPTER 10

From Surviving to Thriving: Reclaiming Myself After Divorce

Laura Richards

I would like to dedicate this chapter to the brave and badass women I have met along the way who have inspired me to use my voice!

Until very recently, I was walking through life unsure of myself and not truly knowing how to find true joy. I used to think that life was nothing exciting and nothing special. I always wondered how others could just be happy in their everyday life. Was that something you were just allowed to be? I felt like I was the only one going through this!

I spent many years in church activities, fun vacations, and outdoor adventures with my husband, and had a lot of good friends. All of these things brought me temporary moments of happiness, but beneath the surface, I struggled with truly understanding who I was in the world.

This all came to a head in 2019 with the health challenges my mother was facing.

2020 was a rough year for our family, as it was for so many of us. My mother passed away after a long illness, we had her funeral, and then we went into lockdown. During that time, I also decided to leave my career as a speech therapist. In 2021, we had another tragedy happen when our sister-in-law passed away from the worldwide virus. The shock of it was too much for our family to bear. Months later I was still understandably sad. I had never grieved like this before. My husband would come home from work and ask me why I was still depressed and crying. Why wasn't I just getting over the two deaths in our family that seemed to him to be so long ago? I agreed with him and decided that going to therapy would be the best thing for me to do, so that I could "get over" my grief.

In therapy I started talking not only about my grief, but why my husband was so difficult. The deaths of my mother and sister-in-law were starting to show me what a truly apathetic person my husband was. For years I had felt like he was difficult, and that everything I did was wrong. I would talk to friends and go to counseling, but nothing ever seemed to help. I really felt like he was a mystery that I needed to solve. Going to individual therapy truly helped me wrap my head around my circumstances, my overall unhappiness, and what I wanted from my life. It was there that I decided that I had had enough of his indifference toward me — 33 years together was more than I could handle.

My therapist provided me with strategies to clearly communicate my emotional needs to him, hopefully helping him understand what I truly needed. I thought it was a ridiculous thing to have to do after 32 years of marriage, but I was still hopeful, and maybe a little delusional, that he would finally get me. Who needs to keep telling their husband of three decades to treat them better? He would sit and listen to the things I had learned in therapy, and things would seem better for a few days. Yet, soon after we were right back where we started.

Over and over in therapy she would say, "You have been exceedingly clear with telling him what you need. He is either unwilling or unable to understand what you need." I finally woke up one day and understood that he was unwilling. Therapy not only gave me the strength to leave my marriage, but it gave me the courage to look at myself and what I wanted out of life. That "just being happy everyday" attitude was still on my mind. I wanted to be one of those people.

I started my healing journey with one focus in mind — who am I as a divorced woman? I needed to heal my broken heart. I needed to know who I was. I needed to learn healthy boundaries. I needed to rewrite the last 33 years.

Laura had no idea who she was. The choices I had made throughout my life were driven by the experiences of my past, including my childhood. As I started to heal, I learned that I really needed to rewrite and heal the last 55 years of my life. The journey was just beginning.

I dove into my journaling, writing down all of my thoughts, hopes, and dreams. I started walking daily to give me the good endorphins to help my mental health. I also slept a lot. As you start to heal after trauma, your nervous system needs to recover, and sleep is often what your body needs. Don't feel bad about those naps! Yes, I said trauma. In the months following my divorce, I discovered that I had, in fact, been in a narcissistic and psychologically abusive marriage.

One weekend, I went to the beach all by myself and stared at the ocean. The ocean is great for so many things, and it has always been a favorite place for me to go. I was proud of myself for taking my therapist's advice to try new things. Going to the beach all by myself was a little nerve-racking, but I was proud of myself for being able to do it. The thoughts in my head were still of "I don't know if I can do things on my own."

As part of my healing journey, I started journaling even these little wins. Little wins are important. We don't need to wait until we've reached a major milestone in our healing journey to celebrate ourselves.

Some days, it was encouraging myself in the mirror for simply getting out of bed. Other days it was patting myself on the back because I met up with a friend for coffee. The little wins are worth celebrating! YOU are worth celebrating!

Thinking back to the time right after my divorce I can say I was sad, but I was proud of the tools I had for my healing. I was doing really well for about three months, and then a bombshell hit. My ex had an issue with inappropriate behavior with other women. It had been a constant battle in our marriage, yet I often let things slide. I feel like I had been trained all my life to not ruffle feathers, and not cause a problem, so I let a lot slide just to keep the peace. People pleasing was something I had learned in childhood, and throughout my life. I learned that if I kept quiet, there wouldn't be any problems. If there weren't any problems, then people would like me! I hoped, anyway! It didn't matter that I felt out of integrity with my actions, I just needed to be liked. It was a deep-seeded need that drove me and all of my actions for many years.

Three months after our divorce, I learned that he had been dating a former coworker. She was someone I suspected he had been seeing but couldn't ever prove. When I found out about her, my entire life flashed before my eyes, and I felt like the blindfold had been ripped off. I suddenly started seeing everything I needed to see about narcissistic abuse! About a year earlier I had heard the word gaslighting, but I wasn't exactly sure what it all meant. He denied gaslighting me when I accused him of it, and I believed him. Ironically, that was all gaslighting! When I heard about narcissistic abuse, all of a sudden my entire marriage made sense. Every lie, every betrayal, every manipulation tactic, every single thing he had said about me, or how he had treated me suddenly became crystal clear. I didn't sleep for three days after I found out about them. Talk about a dysregulated nervous system!

I call this my second Day One! I was devastated, so I dove even deeper into my healing. I now had words and definitions for my pain. Learning about narcissistic abuse helped me to know how to target my healing. Having words for my pain, and reasons for his mind games, helped me to move forward with intention. It was a game of two steps forward, one step back many days, but educating myself helped with the healing process.

As humans, we have a deep need to feel seen and heard. As I learned new terminology, I was able to give names to specific pains. I heard about the trauma bond, cognitive dissonance, and devaluing. While they were painful to hear, learning the terms helped me to wrap my brain around what had happened to me. This helped me feel understood, seen, and heard! The real healing could now begin!

As I was healing, I began looking for support in the community in the form of support groups and talking with friends but was met with opposition. In the church, I was told to forgive and move on. That was a hard pill to swallow when he was walking around scot-free and continuing his abuse. I believe in the power of forgiveness, but did not understand why many support groups jumped to it before helping me understand what had happened to me. I heard a great quote during this time by Glennon Doyle from her book Untamed, "If we cannot forgive and move on, perhaps we need to move on first and forgiveness will follow." I don't want to forgive but I know it is a process I must go through. I hope as I move on forgiveness will follow.

I continued to talk about what happened to me, and I found people who pointed me to resources like Leslie Vernick and Dr. David Clarke who gave me the biblical perspective I needed. In some groups I felt even more shame for having gotten a divorce.

Other people I knew talked to me and told me I shouldn't talk about my ex or call what had happened to me abuse. This was confusing and made me feel very alone. I was too new in my healing and felt ashamed for speaking out about what had happened to me. I wasn't finding a big community of support around me to make me not feel so alone.

When I first found out what had been happening to me for three decades, I felt alone, and that no one understood me. It was so disheartening. Maybe you've felt like that. The statistics show that about 23% of marriages end because of abuse. I can only imagine that the number is bigger, because states like mine are no-fault, and so I never talked about abuse in our divorce mediation meetings. In fact, I didn't even know I had been experiencing abuse when we got divorced!

Even though many people told me not to talk about my abuse, I decided that I just couldn't do that. It didn't make sense to me. If I felt this alone, maybe there were others who felt this alone as well. I wanted to share what I went through with others, so that you can see healing is possible!

I found support in other groups, online, and from other people, including many of my friends, who had been through this very same thing. I learned that people *were* talking about this and there was no shame in doing so! I found many people who gave me the words, support, and hope that I didn't know I needed.

I continued to work on my healing. My heart was understandably broken, so I kept healing through journaling, therapy, and holistic practices. Holistic practices were a new area I'd never dabbled in before, and they have truly helped me so much with dreaming for my future.

I had always loved helping women, and that dream never went away. Soon after my divorce, I employed a friend of mine who is a wellness coach to help me dream again. What did that even mean? I didn't know, but I felt it in my soul. Maybe that's you. Maybe you don't think you'll ever be happy again. I've been there, and I'm proof that you can and will be happy again. I understood the valuable support coaches offer to their clients in helping them move forward in life, and so working with one seemed like the next right step. We really don't have to have it all figured out. We just need to take the right next step to help us on our healing journey. Working with this coach was just the first of many healers who have helped me along the way. As I continue to walk down the path of my healing journey, I talk to new people who can help me gather my thoughts for my next project or season of my life.

When you get a divorce, that does not have to be the ending. It's now the beginning of a wonderful new chapter! As I worked with my coach to help me dream again, I had a newfound freedom to dream as big as I wanted to. In the past I've been limited by the restrictive ideas that my ex-husband had of me. Now I could dream about whatever I wanted to! What I want to dream about I didn't know, and you don't have to know either. Working with a coach is such a freeing process, and they will guide you. I simply want to encourage you to be brave and take that next step toward your future.

I now live my life with freedom in knowing who I am and living as my true self rather than conforming to what others want me to be.

Another thing I started to do was to dabble in holistic healing like meditation and hypnosis. I had never tried hypnosis before, and it really helped with the deep healing work I truly needed. I have learned through my healing journey that healing the inner child was instrumental for me, and it helped me learn healthy boundaries. Boundaries were not something I had really had in my life, but now was instrumental in moving forward.

During the time I dreamt with my coach, I felt the need to create a community for women who were like me who felt alone in their journey after divorce. I dreamt of my podcast and started talking to women all over the world about how they have healed. As I recorded episodes and did interviews on other shows, I came to a realization. I started a podcast because I felt like no one ever listened to me! That was eye-opening!

As I was healing, I learned another hard truth. As I learned to set boundaries, I had friends who didn't come around anymore. It was a big shock to me, but the truth is that when you learn to set boundaries, those who benefited from you not having boundaries will be your harshest critics. Do not take that as a sign to not set boundaries. You have to think about your mental health first before anything else.

The more I recorded and interviewed, the more I learned that I loved giving women a voice to talk about the things that society deems unacceptable to talk about. No longer would we be quiet about the abuse that had happened to us.

Almost two years after my divorce I wrote a book about being married to and divorcing a "nice" guy. Nice guy is what everyone thought of my ex. In public he was the nicest guy, serving the homeless, and stopping whatever he was doing to help a stranger. At home, it was different. It was really hard to reconcile that until I learned that this is the way narcissists behave. I now let the world know what narcissists do, so that they won't be manipulated by their tactics. I share with you what I went through, so that you won't have to go through it!

My podcast is a hit, and my book is a best seller. Those things are fun, but my mission is where I keep my focus: to shine a light on narcissistic abuse and let women know they are never alone, and that healing is always possible.

As you heal, what will you find to be your mission in life? Perhaps it's to be a grand example of someone who felt like they lost just about everything but is now thriving. Thriving, not just surviving, in your happiness, in your career, and in your life is possible! It's not only possible, but you are worthy of true happiness!

I've been at rock bottom, just like perhaps you have, and I am on the other side where hope and healing live. I live where my true self comes out to shine, so others can know that there is hope. What will you do today to get to where you want to be? What is the next right step you need to take for your life?

No matter how low you feel, don't give up. It gets better from here! There is freedom in knowing your true worth and value and living as your true self!

It doesn't matter what you've been through, you can thrive after divorce!

Laura Richards

Laura Richards is an international podcaster, #1 bestselling author, and speaker dedicated to empowering women. Through her global podcast, "That's Where I'm At," and her bestselling book "*Married to A "Nice" Guy: Getting Over Narcissistic Abuse*," Laura shares her personal journey of recovery from a 32-year marriage to a narcissist.

Drawing from her own experiences, Laura's mission is simple: to shine a light on narcissistic abuse and let women know they are never alone, and that healing is always possible. With warmth, authenticity, and an unwavering commitment to truth, Laura helps women rebuild their self-worth, reclaim their voices, and step into a future filled with confidence and strength.

She is the mom of three grown children, a mother-in-law, and a grandmother who lives happily with her cat in her hometown of Las Vegas.

Connect with Laura at https://www.thatswhereimatpodcast.com.

CHAPTER 11
Phoenix Rising

Lesley Evans

---

*For all the women who have said they want more but don't
know what it is yet.
For all the women starting to figure it out.
Dedicated to all the women who are thinking they want
more but haven't said it out loud yet.*

My story begins with a checklist—the kind you create when you're young, filled with all the dreams and goals you envision for your future.

I graduated from psychiatric nursing - check.

I got a job in public health - check.

I married my college sweetheart - check.

We bought a house - check.

We had three beautiful girls - check check check.

I was primary support to my mom, and I created this life that I thought I wanted. You might know that life, the one that when you were young seemed like everything you wanted.

As the years went by, I lost myself to that checklist. I was busy trying to make sure everybody was happy, trying to be the mental health therapist that helped everybody to get back on their feet, no matter how busy it became at work. I was the mom that just wanted to be there for my girls, and the wife that tried to make her husband happy.

…and as the years went by, I lost myself to that checklist. See? The checklist became way more important than I was.

I felt like I had everything that I ever wanted. So why was I so unhappy? Why were things not going the way that they were supposed to go? And why was I not satisfied?

One day when I was having a conversation with my eldest, it came to me. She was 16 at the time and we were talking about a boy that she was having troubles with. She had given up the things she loved, like dancing and singing, hanging out with her friends and started to do things that she wouldn't normally do to be with this boy. I gave her the great motherly advice… If they care about you, they'll support you and encourage you to do all those things you love. They won't ask you not to attend them.

A light bulb went off in my head. I had to take a really good look at myself. It really made me think I thought I was teaching my girls that they were the most important thing in the world… and they knew to me they were. What I was also teaching them was that when you love someone you go last. That's not what I wanted for my girls. I wanted my girls to understand that they are as important as the people that they love, that their dreams and aspirations and their passions are just as important, and I wanted them to live their lives full of passion and inspiration. Here I was modeling to them that you go last, after all those important people in your life.

So I went home after that chat and I had a good little chat with myself. I decided it was time to make some changes. I wanted to be a better model to my children — so I did.

I left a marriage of 21 years. More than half my life was spent in that relationship, and I moved out into a home with my girls and my mom to make a new life for us. It was a huge turning point.

But as the separation went on, I began to worry about everyone around me again, how my girls were doing with the transition. I worried about my mom, who just lost her mom, and worried about her transition. And I worried about my clients at work making sure everybody was doing okay. One day, something shifted—I'm not sure what exactly it was. All I know is that I went home for lunch, and by the time I returned, something else had happened that felt like the proverbial straw that broke the camel's back. I clearly remember driving back to work for my final three and a quarter hours in urgent mental health, where I was helping people in crisis. As I parked and took a deep breath, I resolved to give it my all and be the best therapist I could be. And I did. I poured everything into helping those in need during my shift.

At the end of those three and a quarter hours, I took another deep breath and started to gather my things. That's when I noticed something was wrong—I couldn't find my keys. They weren't in my purse, coat pocket, or drawer. I searched every usual spot, but they were nowhere to be found. I remember thinking to myself, "Well, I really hope my car's still out there."

As I walked out to the parking lot, I scanned for my car, and there it was—still right where I'd parked it. But that wasn't the surprising part. My car had been running for the entire three and a half hours of my shift. I climbed in, turned it off, and just sat there for a moment, unsure why I had left it running in the first place. At the time, it somehow seemed like a good idea. Taking a deep breath, I rested my head on the steering wheel, and at that moment, it hit me—I felt as empty as my now-depleted gas tank.

As I drove home on that nearly empty tank of gas, I made a decision: it was time for a change. I needed to change for myself, and I needed to change for my daughters. I wanted them to understand their worth, and the best way to teach them that was by showing them their mother learning to recognize and embrace her own worth.

So, I began making changes—small but necessary steps—because I knew I needed to, not just for myself, but for my daughters and the people I worked with. It wasn't a quick process, nor should it have been. Building a solid foundation for myself took time and intention.

I started by exploring the things that brought me joy. I discovered the foods I loved to eat, the activities that made me feel alive, and surrounded myself with new friends who uplifted and inspired me. Each small choice I made for myself led to a deeper understanding that life was far richer and more expansive than what I had previously allowed myself to see.

As I opened myself to these new possibilities, I began connecting with more people who resonated with my journey. The more I sought out this deeper meaning, the more I found a sense of belonging and fulfillment that I hadn't known was possible.

I found a little school called the Home of Om in my home city, where I started to connect with alternative therapies. You see, by that time I'd been a therapist for over 20 years, and the things that I had in my toolbox to help the people that I worked with definitely were helping me, but I needed more. As I searched for more, I understood that the only true way to heal was to heal on all levels from a conscious level, from a subconscious level, and from a soul level.

As I continued to grow and connect with people who shared a similar vision, I began to uncover deeper truths about myself. A few significant realizations emerged.

I came to understand that I was truly worthy—worthy of living a life I desired, a life that filled me with passion and inspiration. I realized I deserved to create a life that encompassed everything I could ever want, and that it wasn't just a dream but something I had the power to make a reality. This understanding became the foundation for the life I began to build.

And as I understood that worthiness, I began to reach for more, and when I was ready, I reached out and found my soul partner, best friend, greatest support and love of my life. I was ready to understand that whatever partner I chose, and who chose me, required that we were equal, and that we supported each other's dreams, and that we do.

And then I understood that I wanted more than working in the public health system because I wasn't helping people to the depth that I know they need. So I began my own private practice as a therapist, as a hypnotherapist, and as an Akashic guide. I now help people heal and create the life they truly want from that conscious, subconscious and soul level healing that's profound and lasting.

My private practice allows me to create in the way I want, and to have the lifestyle that I want. I plan my own schedule and go on vacations when we want.

At the time, letting go of my checklist felt devastating, as if I were abandoning a part of myself. Yet, in time, it became a source of hope and healing. There were moments when it was incredibly difficult to see beyond the pain, anger, disappointment, and even my own reactions. But deep down, I knew one thing for certain: I wanted to be proud of how I faced life's challenges. I wanted to stay true to myself, and for the most part, I did just that.

If you're navigating this journey, or if you're contemplating navigating this journey, just know that there is light in that tunnel, things will get better.

Know this, it is of utmost importance to put yourself as a priority. It is not an option. It is absolutely necessary to take time for yourself whether you have children or not. Because, as you heal, those around you also heal. By you healing, you create a space and give them permission to heal too.

Lesley Evans

Lesley Evans is International Speaker and Best-Selling Author of De-FUNK YourSELF. She has developed a perfect blend of modern and magical therapies to empower women to give themselves permission to be limitless and unlock endless possibilities.

Lesley has 30 years of experience as a Registered Psychiatric Nurse Therapist. She is a Clinical Hypnotherapist, Certified Soul Care Practitioner and Reiki Master. She brings new purpose and passion for raising awareness, gaining new perspectives and teaching others to Shine Their Light. She believes, like The Rising Phoenix, that everyone can rise from the ashes of their old life and build themselves stronger to shine their light into the world.

Connect with Lesley at https://www.riseofthephoenix.org.

CHAPTER 12
From Fear to Formidable

Lori L. Danecke

My journey to divorce began the day I got married!

I was sitting in the back seat of the limousine in the church parking lot when I knew I didn't want to get married. Obviously I did; otherwise, I wouldn't be divorced. There was a little voice inside of me that was begging me not to get out of the limo. When I told my mom that I didn't want to do this, she commanded me to get out of the car and into the church because people were waiting, and expecting a wedding. Who was I to disappoint anyone?!

You see, I have done everything that was expected of me and con-sidered acceptable all my life. I was a people-pleaser! If everyone was happy then I was happy, or so I believed.

I graduated from high school, went to University, got a job, got married, bought a house and had kids. I grew up being told that is what normal people do, and society expects us to do, so that's what I did. Don't get me wrong, I love my two boys, my daughters-in-law and my four beautiful grandchildren and I wouldn't trade them for the world and—it all came at the cost of losing myself in the process.

My now ex-husband is a kind and gentle man and the clues were there before we got married; however, I chose unconsciously to ignore them.

The conversations we had were without depth, short and infrequent as time passed. When we talked at the dinner table, it was how was your day and that's about it or about how much money we had in the bank. We lived on separate floors of the house for over 10 years. I felt alone, rejected, unheard, unseen, and unloved. This created a lot of an-ger inside that was eating me alive. I didn't realize at the time that I was dying inside. The best way to describe it is that when I was home by myself I felt alone, angry and scared. When he was home, I felt lonely, sad and hurt! There was little to no affection and I was successful at putting up a front with family and friends of us being a happy couple.

The longer I stayed, the worse I felt about myself to the point where I hated who I was and what I had become. I was living a lie and didn't know a way out without hurting anyone. I betrayed myself in so many ways that resulted in a deep depression.

I chose to stay because I had no confidence in myself and I felt stuck where I was and believed that I had no options, especially since I was financially dependent on him.

February 2, 2022, is a day I will never forget. It was the day I stepped into the first day of the rest of my life! It was the scariest and the most empowering day I've ever experienced.

That day was the culmination of 35+ years of feeling alone, rejected, unheard, unseen, unloved, fear, anger, sadness, guilt and shame.

Have you ever experienced any or all of these negative thoughts and emotions?

I love the game of golf and that became my refuge. I played as often as I could. I was able to do this because I volunteered at a local course in exchange for a full golf membership. It was a great option for me because it didn't cost any money; therefore, he had nothing to gripe about (as far as money goes at least). He wanted me to get a full-time job now that the boys were away at college and university. He began to resent the fact that I wasn't bringing home any money even though I pretty much stayed home and raised the boys and supported them with everything they did. I did start my own house painting company before the golf opportunity came along and that wasn't good enough for him. He wanted me to work full time and I didn't believe there was a job out there that, for one thing, I'd even have the qualifications necessary because I hadn't been working for at least 10 years.

Back to golf! As I said earlier, golf had become a refuge for me. It was one of the places I felt I could be me until my home life began to invade my golf life and I carried my anger and resentment to the course. As you may or may not know, your golf game is a direct reflection on what is going on in your life. I became the angry, frustrated, club slamming, cussing golfer! I wasn't having fun anymore and I'm sure my playing partners weren't having much fun playing with me either. This just added to the degree that I hated myself!

Then when I had had enough and was going to quit playing, I came across an opportunity that changed everything for me. The Universe delivers exactly what we need even when we have no clue what it is that we need or want because we feel so lost!

I took a five-day class that was centered on the golf mindset because I had a goal of winning the club championship. It not only saved my golf game, but it also saved my life! The class taught me the skills and started to create the belief that I deserved better not just on the golf course, but in my life. I dedicated myself to practicing not only the skills of the game but the power of the mind. The game of golf is 90% mindset and 10% skills.

The more I implemented these tools the better I felt, and it became the springboard for real change for me. The game of golf truly saved me!

I won the championship that season and the rest is history. My entire life changed. As I became more confident and gained more belief in myself, the more I changed. What happened next was incredibly profound. I came to the realization that I deserved better than the life I was living. It was such a demeaning and debilitating place for me that I knew something needed change.

I worked with that coach who put on that class to dig into where all the lack of belief in myself started and released a lot of negative thoughts, beliefs and emotions that were holding me hostage in all areas of my life using the tools that I am now utilizing for my clients in my coaching business—Impact Your Life Coaching

Through this process, I discovered a part of me that I had buried for decades. I found a confident, self-assured woman, secure in who I was and where I wanted to go and what I wanted to do!

There was a moment of brief hesitation before I made the boldest move I have ever made! It was February 2, 2022 and I made the decision that it was time to put myself first knowing it was not only the best decision for me, but for everyone involved.

I was nervous and a little scared. I knew that I deserved to live my life as I wanted, what was best for me and not for everyone else. It was the most selfless thing I've ever done. I was tired and exhausted from doing everything for everyone else, so I asked for what I wanted and needed, a DIVORCE!

I had packed my car and was ready to go and there was nothing and no one that could change my mind. All that was left was to have what could be a difficult and uncomfortable conversation.

When I took that last deep breath, I said what I needed to say with a self-assuredness and inner strength I hadn't experienced in a very long time. I did feel bad for him because I caught him totally off guard, although I was dumbfounded that he didn't see it coming since we had had a heated discussion a couple months earlier when I gave him a choice, whether he wanted to work on our marriage or not. I never got an answer to that question. I took no answer as the answer, that he either didn't care enough to fix it or didn't think there was a problem and that is when I made the decision that I had to put myself first and take whatever actions necessary to do the things that were best for me.

I felt a great sense of empowerment that I had put myself first and was secure that I had made the right decision for me.

I had been doing a lot more mindset work up to that moment and still am doing the work for myself and also for others. I got my first coaching/practitioner certification in October 2021. That is where I had a vision of what I wanted to do and how. I didn't understand it at the time because it seemed SO farfetched from the life I was living at the time. I knew back then that there was more to life than a money based transactional marriage. I just didn't know or understand that I had within me the whole time the strength to leave!

Seven weeks after I left, I purchased an RV that I had envisioned and fulfilled my vision of travelling around Canada and the United States on my own! The RV represented the freedom I had been seeking all along.

I met a lot of people and have so many experiences that never would have happened if I stayed in my marriage. There were moments of doubt and even some fear, yet the feeling of independence far outweighed any doubt that crept in. Part of that vision was to arrive at my next level of coaching training and certification at the Master level in my RV. It was surreal when I pulled into the event parking lot in California. It happened exactly as I had envisioned! I still pinch myself every once in a while, and realize how far I have come.

I have created the life I desire and deserve with the support of an amazing community that I know now was created to help me get where I needed and wanted to go and build back my inner strength and fortitude. I continue to learn, grow and expand through meditation, receiving and providing coaching to others. I continue to hone myself and my craft with several advanced training, doing workshops and providing all those opportunities for others, especially women!

I have created and continue to create the life I desire and deserve. I have my sense of wonderment and adventure back that I had lost as a young girl. There were glimpses every once in a while, like the time I went on a three-week jaunt around Europe on my own after graduating from university where I explored five countries.

It has been through my recent travels around the world that I rediscovered a strength and independence that I didn't know existed within me. I have been to parts of the world I never thought were possible because I had set that dream aside and forgot about it until I started working on myself and my mindset with a great support system that let me fail without judgment. They supported me and pushed me up against my limiting beliefs.

I have been to Kenya, Spain, Mexico, and I just got back from a spiritual retreat in Bali! These experiences supported me and pushed me up against my limiting beliefs to discover how amazing I am and I continue to work on myself while I support my clients to break through their patterns that are no longer serving them by releasing their negative thoughts, emotions and beliefs they have suppressed since childhood. This allows them to free themselves to live the life they deserve and desire so they can flourish as I have and will continue to flourish until the end of time. I have created connections and met people I never would have the pleasure of experiencing if I had stayed. My family and friends have supported me throughout my new journey, and I have made so many more connections. That never would have happened if I hadn't stepped into the courageous part of me despite the fear that creeps in every now and then. I truly believe that every person deserves to have a coach; even coaches need coaches.

I had a dream, wish, desire (whatever you want to call it) when I was 12 years old while I was camping with my mom and brother in the Banff area of Alberta Canada when I told my mom that I was going to live in British Columbia one day. Well, 48 years later, I arrived in my RV and have now settled into my own place. I still have the RV and have loved exploring other parts of the province in it. My oldest son lives close by with his family and it brings me great joy and laughter when I hang out with them, especially my grandkids. I travel back to Ontario regularly to visit the rest of my family and have more fun and laughter with my grandkids who live there.

The things and people I have experienced over the last two years blow my mind (in a great way)!

My whole journey over the last 3.5 years has been one of growth and change. It has not always been easy; there have been highs, lows and everything in between. Now, though, I'm so much better equipped to handle the ebbs and flows with grace and integrity. I'm a completely different person now, one that I love. My relationships with my family, friends and myself are on a strong foundation of love, understanding and compassion.

Because of my love for myself and growth I have experienced, I have created a new standard for healthy boundaries for myself and I practice those boundaries with others and respect their boundaries without judgment. Before this shift and growth of my inner strength, my boundaries were blurred and unclear. Now they are solid and practiced.

One thing I'm looking forward to adding back in my life is my inner artist. I loved creating art of all kinds, especially painting. I now have all of my art supplies with me and will be setting up a space in my new place where I can get the creative juices flowing again.

I have a partner who loves all of me and loves and understands the kind of work I do with my clients. She was open to experiencing these tools and techniques with a fellow coach and our relationship has benefitted so much from this mutual respect we have for each other's quirks and all that we are. She has allowed me to be my authentic self like no one else has before. I have learned to understand my flaws and weaknesses and accept them for what they are while simultaneously taking steps towards moving forward to move them up the scale and into strengths. Yes, it will take some work and coaching and I'm open to more growth and changes while accepting whatever comes my way. Everything is an opportunity to grow and expand.

My relationship with myself is the best it has ever been and I'm looking forward to even more forward movement and growth. It's not always going to be easy AND it will be worth every second.

I've gone from full of doubt to confidence, from hating myself to loving myself, from hiding and scared to bold and self-assured. I can hardly wait to experience what life has in store for me next. I'm ready!!

I want this for every person in the world! Are you ready?

REMEMBER this one thing: no matter your current circumstances, no matter your gender or how old you are, you deserve to live the life you think and dream about:

IT'S NEVER TOO LATE to go from FEAR TO FORMIDABLE!!!!

Lori Danecke

Lori Danecke is a dynamic force in the world of personal transformation and empowerment. As the Creator and CEO of Impact Your Life Coaching, Lori specializes in guiding individuals to break free from limiting beliefs and unlock their full potential.

With certifications as a Master Certified Coach and Practitioner in NLP (Neuro-Linguistic Programming), Quantum Release Process, Hypnotherapy, and Reiki, Lori integrates powerful modalities to create lasting change. She also practices Huna Energy Releases, an ancient Hawaiian healing tradition, and holds certifications in Trauma and PTSD recovery, making her uniquely equipped to support clients through life's toughest challenges.

Beyond her professional accolades, Lori is a proud mother of two sons, two daughters-in-law, and a loving grandmother to four grandchildren. She is also a 2-time Canadian and World Long Drive Champion in the 60+ Women's division, embodying the resilience and determination she inspires in her clients.

Lori's mission is clear: to help others heal, thrive, and create meaningful impact in their lives.

Connect with Lori at loridanecke@gmail.com.

CHAPTER 13

From Shadow to Sunshine: Finding Light After Darkness

Lynda Sunshine West

I dedicate this chapter to every woman who is faced with fear of leaving her current situation. Trust me, with the right people in your corner, leaving can be the right and best decision you'll ever make.

"I didn't know I was in the dark until I was in the light.."
~Lynda Sunshine West

In every life, there are defining moments that carve paths we never planned to tread. Mine was no different.

As a young woman, I found myself entangled in an abusive marriage, bound by fear and a desperate hope for a better future. This chapter is a testament to the power of transformation—a journey from the depths of despair to the heights of empowerment. It is about breaking chains, confronting fears, and discovering an unyielding strength that propels us forward. Through my story, I hope to illuminate the path for others who find themselves in the shadow of their darkest moments, to show that it is not just possible to survive, but to thrive and transform adversity into opportunity.

Marriage and Breakup

At 19 years old, life seemed a canvas of immense possibilities, yet tinged by the shadows of a tumultuous family life. Raised under the roof of a volatile, abusive alcoholic father, my understanding of relationships was skewed by the echoes of my mother's silent sacrifices. She was the ultimate enabler due to her fear of "what will happen if I do… or say…." So, when I met my first husband, I was swayed not by love, but by a compulsion to adhere to the rigid expectations set by my family. Pregnant and pressured, I married in haste, driven by a desperate hope to shield my father from the truth of my premarital pregnancy and to perhaps carve out a happier existence than my mother's. My sole expectation from the marriage was to find kindness and support—a partner who would rewrite the narrative of fear and subjugation that had colored my upbringing.

However, the hope for a nurturing partnership quickly dissolved into the grim reality of living with an abusive spouse. I was repeating my mom's life. That isn't what I wanted for my life. I wanted a better life.

Echoing the patterns I had witnessed as a child, my husband's daily tirades became a dark refrain that undercut my confidence and self-worth. His words, "You're so stupid. You're so ignorant. People are only nice to you because they feel sorry for you," were not just remarks but chisels, each day carving away a little more of my self-esteem. I began to believe him, to see myself through the distorted lens he held up to me. This relentless emotional abuse left me questioning my intelligence, my value, and my potential to ever lead a life different from my mother's—a life I had once imagined as one filled with love and respect.

The turning point was both subtle and seismic. Each day, as he drove me to work, my husband's verbal lashings were the prelude to silent tears wiped away in the solitude of a credit union parking lot. Despite holding a position of authority at work, the irony of my supposed power contrasted sharply with the helplessness I felt at home.

The decision to leave my ex was not sparked by a singular outburst, but rather by a creeping realization that my two paths—stay or go—were both paved with fear. Staying meant consigning myself and my children (my daughter only four weeks old and my son only 14 months old) to a cycle of abuse, repeating my mother's history. Leaving was terrifying, an unknown fraught with challenges, especially with two young children in tow.

Yet, in that moment of profound fear, after two of the longest years of my entire life, I chose the path that held a glimmer of hope over certain despair. One fear-laden day, with a baby carrier in one hand, my son on my hip, a diaper bag over one shoulder, and my purse over the other, I walked away from my abusive marriage (literally "walked" away because I didn't have a car), stepping into uncertainty yet driven by the promise of reclaiming my life and forging a better future for me and my children.

Struggles with Financial Burdens and Logistical Issues

Leaving my abusive marriage was just the beginning of a long journey fraught with immediate and pressing challenges. The shackles of my past were not just emotional but also financial. My ex-husband remained in our apartment, a space that no longer felt like home to me, yet one for which I was still wholly financially responsible. He contributed nothing towards the rent, utilities, or even the car payments, all of which were in my name. His refusal to shoulder any part of our mutual obligations left me burdened with debts and ongoing expenses, despite no longer living there. The struggle was not just about making ends meet; it was about preventing financial ruin while trying to provide a stable environment for my two young children.

I was totally embarrassed the day my boss at the credit union came to me and said, "I need you to give me your credit card. You are way over your limit and the credit union has requested you give up your card." Since I never used our credit card, I had no idea we were over our limit. My now-ex spent more than double our credit card limit. Back in the 1980s, you could charge your card and the bank wouldn't know for a few days. So, if you went over your limit, you could keep charging on your card until it finally caught up with you. Well, it caught up to us and my card was taken away from me.

Emotional and Practical Steps Toward Rebuilding an Independent Life

Emotionally drained yet determined, I set about reconstructing my life from the ruins left by my marriage. The first practical step was to secure a new living situation where my children and I could feel safe and start anew. Securing a new home was daunting, compounded by my financial strains, but it was essential for our emotional and physical safety. I also began to reevaluate my career options, looking for ways to enhance my income. This period was marked by a series of small but significant victories—each bill paid and each night of peace was a step away from my past torment. I not only had my own bills, but I was also paying my ex's bills that he racked up because they were in my name and I was trying hard to preserve my credit.

Meeting Wheatie: A New Beginning

Three years after my divorce, a new chapter began with Scott aka Wheatie. We were introduced by mutual friends. When I met him, I was twitterpated and felt like he was the one. My children, then three and four, took to him immediately, my daughter especially smitten. Wheatie's presence brought a new kind of light into our lives, one filled with the promise of happiness and genuine care. We started dating right away, and as our relationship developed, so did the realization that life could indeed offer the kindness I once hoped to find.

Initially, though, I struggled with feelings of unworthiness, haunted by the shadows of my past abuses that questioned my right to happiness. Wheatie's steadfast kindness and patience gradually warmed my heart to the idea that I did deserve someone good, someone who genuinely cared. As I allowed myself to accept this happiness, our relationship deepened, teaching me the true meaning of mutual support and love.

Decades after meeting and marrying Wheatie, I decided to embark on an emotional journey to reclaim my sense of self. This involved a lot of introspective work, where I had to unlearn the falsehoods imprinted on me by years of abuse. I found a life coach and slowly started to peel away the layers of fear and self-doubt that had built up over the years. It was a time of profound personal struggle, but also of gradual empowerment as I learned to stand on my own, free from the shadow of my ex-husband's belittlement.

Each step forward was hard-won, but with each stride, I grew stronger, more independent, and more determined to create a life of peace and stability for myself and my children. This phase of my life was less about immediate recovery and more about laying a new foundation on which a brighter future could be built.

As my entrepreneurial spirit took flight, it brought unforeseen challenges to our loving marriage. My drive and evolving ambitions seemed to eclipse the person Wheatie had married, stirring feelings of redundancy and confusion in him. The intensity of my entrepreneurial goals and personal development at times made him feel unneeded, a difficult realization for someone who values being a pillar of support. Facing these marital strains, Wheatie actually considered divorcing me because we were "growing apart" as I was stepping into my own person. I was a people-pleaser for 51 years and, because of that, I didn't know who I was. My life coach helped me to evolve and realize who I am, what I like and dislike, who I want to be, what I want to do with the rest of my life, and so much more.

Fortunately, Wheatie and I sat down and talked about our future together, and we learned to communicate more profoundly, leading me to reassure him, "I don't need you, but I want you. Isn't that better?" This understanding helped us navigate through the storm, emerging stronger and more in love.

I'm grateful that we spent time talking about all of this because I love him so much and didn't want to lose him, but I also didn't want to go back to being the people-pleasing person I had worked so hard to leave behind. That one conversation was probably the most important conversation we have ever had in 36 years of marriage.

A Year of Transformation: Breaking Through Fears

At the age of 51, I came to the conclusion that fear was holding me back from living the life I truly want to live, and I wanted to do something about it. So, I decided to embark on a daring challenge to confront one fear every day for an entire year, 365 days in a row. This journey was not just about overcoming fears but about transforming my fears into steppingstones towards personal empowerment. Each day presented a new battle and a new victory, profoundly reshaping my approach to life and self-belief.

Each day of overcoming a fear was akin to adding a single drop of water to a bucket. At first, these drops seemed inconsequential, barely covering the bottom. Public speaking added one drop, asserting myself in professional settings another, and tackling personal insecurities yet another. Each fear faced, each drop added, seemed small on its own, but over time, these drops accumulated. The bucket that once appeared empty began to fill, each drop resonating with the echoes of the last, creating ripples that grew larger and stronger.

By the end of the year, the bucket was not only full but overflowing. This wasn't just water in a bucket anymore; it had transformed into a dynamic force, much like a reservoir ready to nourish fields that were once parched. This reservoir of courage, built drop by drop from conquered fears, now had the power to irrigate new dreams, ambitions, and opportunities, turning once barren lands into fertile grounds for growth and success.

The culmination of this transformative year was the birth of Action Takers Publishing. Inspired by my journey and the stories of resilience I encountered along the way, I was driven to create a platform that empowered others to share their stories, turning personal challenges into opportunities for growth and impact.

The Role of Perseverance in Overcoming Personal and Professional Challenges

One of the vital lessons my journey has taught me is that perseverance is not merely about enduring but about persisting with a purpose, with an eye towards growth and achievement. Each setback faced and overcome has fortified my resolve, like steel tempered in fire, making it stronger and more resilient.

This process of overcoming has not just built my character but has also honed my vision for what I wanted to achieve, both personally and professionally. Through the challenges, I have learned to channel my energies more effectively, focusing on goals that align with my deepest values and ambitions. The road was fraught with hurdles, yet each one was a opportunity to climb higher and see further, shaping a path laden with learned wisdom and newfound determination.

Yet, even as I built this path of perseverance brick by brick, I was never alone in my endeavors. The journey, marked by its trials and triumphs, was profoundly shared. Just as a tree might grow strong and tall, its roots are fed not only by the soil of its own planting but also by the waters brought forth by surrounding streams.

No journey is solitary, and mine was no exception. The support from mentors and coaches, alongside Wheatie's unwavering moral support, provided me with the strength to continue pushing boundaries. Like navigators in the uncharted waters of my challenges, their guidance was instrumental in helping me steer through the darkest times and in recognizing the milestones worthy of celebration. Each piece of advice, each supportive gesture, was like a bright light during the storms, ensuring that I remained on course towards my dreams. Their belief in my potential and their readiness to stand by me transformed what could have been a solitary fight into a collaborative journey towards success and fulfillment.

Personal Strengths Developed Through Overcoming Divorce and Fears

Reflecting on my past, I see a tapestry of trials and triumphs that have imbued me with an indomitable strength and a deep empathy for others facing similar battles. These experiences have prepared me for ongoing and future challenges, equipping me with the resilience and wisdom to tackle them head-on.

The lessons learned have not only prepared me for the challenges but have also opened doors to opportunities that I could never have imagined. They have shaped my approach to business, leadership, and personal relationships, reinforcing the belief that every challenge carries the seed of an equal or greater benefit. These experiences have taught me that adversity is not just a barrier but a doorway to new paths, each with the potential to lead somewhere extraordinary, somewhere I might never have reached had I not faced and overcome the challenges before me.

This understanding is encapsulated in the guiding principles that have lit up my journey and which I share in the hope of lighting the way for others:

"Be brave and share your weaknesses, for in your weaknesses, others see your strength."
~Lynda Sunshine West

This speaks to the paradoxical power found in vulnerability—how our greatest growth often sprouts from what we fear to reveal.

"Everything you want is on the other side of your comfort zone. Step outside of it to see what's there, then keep moving forward to get the prize." ~Lynda Sunshine West

---

This is a call to action, urging us to venture beyond the familiar to grasp the possibilities that await.

"Do It BECAUSE You're Scared." ~Lynda Sunshine West

This is my favorite mantra because it turns fear on its head, transforming it from a stop sign into a go signal, pushing us towards rather than away from our potential.

You see, one of my greatest lessons in life was the year I was breaking through fears 365 days in a row. I learned that the vast majority of time when we break through fears, the results are amazing. So, if the results are amazing the vast majority of the time, why do we deprive ourselves of those great results? For this reason alone, we MUST do it BECAUSE we're scared. No more depriving yourself of what is possible on the other side of fear. Get yourself out there and Do It BECAUSE You're Scared. You'll be glad you did (well, at least most of the time).

My first marriage has indeed shaped me, but it does not confine me to that shape for the rest of my life. It has created within me a sense of compassion and a readiness to help those who are still finding their way out of the darkness.

Life's transformative journeys begin when we are ready to see the guides waiting to help us. There's a saying that, "When the student is ready, the teacher will appear." I've realized that the teacher is always there; it's the student who must be ready.

Just as I found guidance in the way of a life coach when I was prepared to change, I hope to serve as a guide for others, illuminating their paths toward personal growth and fulfillment through encouragement.

Know this: when you're ready to open up and learn about yourself on a deep and intimate level, there will always be someone waiting to guide you and show you the way. Often, just sharing your own story, as I have done here, can bring healing and happiness. When you're ready to take that step, I'll be here to welcome you.

Lynda Sunshine West

Lynda Sunshine West is the Founder & CEO of Action Takers Publishing, a women-owned business based in San Diego, California. With a mission to empower 5 million women and men to share their stories with the world, Lynda Sunshine specializes in helping authors use their books as powerful marketing tools to elevate their brands and create lasting impact. Her expertise lies in collaborative book projects, working with visionary leaders to bring their communities together and amplify their voices through shared storytelling. Action Takers Publishing donates to nonprofit organizations, exemplifying Lynda Sunshine's commitment to making a difference.

Outside of her professional achievements, Lynda Sunshine's personal story is one of resilience and transformation. She ran away from home at just five years old, a pivotal event that left her riddled with fears and a tendency toward people-pleasing. At age 51, she faced her fears head-on, breaking through one fear a day for an entire year. This life-changing journey inspired her mantra, "Do It BECAUSE You're Scared," which is also the title of her groundbreaking book.

In her downtime, Lynda Sunshine enjoys playing bass guitar and singing in a rock band, a skill she picked up at 47, proving it's never too late to start something new. She also loves hosting retreats, speaking on breaking through fear, and supporting others in stepping into their power. With her infectious energy and deep passion for storytelling, Lynda Sunshine is on a mission to help people turn their dreams into action and their stories into legacies.

Connect with Lynda Sunshine at

www.ActionTakersPublishing.com.

CHAPTER 14

RISE: Lessons in Divorce from a Mom of Children with Special Needs

Mary Ann Pano Hughes

*I dedicate this chapter to all the moms of kids with special
needs who advocate for their children every day,
in divorce and in life.*

I never imagined I would be divorced. Nor did I ever imagine I would be the mother of children with autism. But both of these things became my reality, which led me to the incredible journey I am on today.

I love both of my children deeply, two wonderful boys who are on opposite ends of the autism spectrum. This mean that means their skills and challenges are quite varied, and that, as their mom, caregiver, advocate, and biggest fan, I'm addressing a variety of needs on a daily basis.

It was a team effort by both parents, jointly participating in raising and supporting the children, with Mom having primary caregiving responsibilities, and Dad being the primary financial provider for the family. This seemed to work, we seemed happy, until one day I discovered that wasn't the case at all…

After 21 years of marriage, I found myself facing divorce. Though it was not something I expected or saw coming, I knew I had to focus on my children throughout the process to ensure that they would feel safe and loved and have their needs met in the short term as well as the long term. Emotional and financial security is what we all want for our kids, but being the mom of autistic children with ongoing support needs, I instinctively knew I had to take extra steps to make sure I approached and made decisions in my divorce to ensure my children's future well-being.

It was hard to find resources and professionals who were knowledgeable and experienced in working with families who had children with autism to help me in this process. This was very frustrating and discouraging, especially with the high incidence of divorce among special needs families. But I didn't let that stop me. I came up with ways to support my kids, and I was able to create a team of professionals who helped me advocate for my children.

I'm proud to share that my hard work did pay off in terms of a good outcome in divorce for my children, but I didn't want all the time, money and energy I spent on my divorce to go to waste. I didn't think it was right that other parents who were facing similar challenges should have to recreate the wheel to find resources in their own special needs divorce. So, I made it my mission to support other parents of children with disabilities navigating divorce and transition challenges. That's when I started Special Family Transitions and started my journey to becoming a Special Needs Divorce Coach.

Prior to my divorce journey, I never considered starting my own business. In fact, I had been a stay-at-home mom for about 20 years, since my eldest child was born. I did work before I had children, with an MBA and employment at several Fortune 500 companies. I expected to return to work, and being able to balance and excelling at being a wife and working mom. But with the autism diagnoses for my kids, my life took a different path.

I had always been an ambitious person, wanting to make a difference in the world. However, my focus over the years became supporting and advocating for my children. Not that I regret a moment of that precious time, but looking back on those years, I realize I lost sight of who I was, and what I was capable of, beyond just being a wife, mom, and homemaker.

Though I wouldn't wish divorce upon anyone, if it wasn't for my divorce, I wouldn't be who I am today, the confident person I was when I was young, ready to take on the world. I may be even more confident now, not just because I'm older and wiser, but because I have learned so many things along the way about life, myself, and those around me.

My divorce presented an opportunity to reexamine what is important to me, who is important to me, and who has my best interest at heart. Sometimes situations or people that we believed to be true actually were not what we made them out to be. Divorce lets us see things and people more clearly. This is not to say we have to become cynics, but our eyes, mind and heart can now accept the reality of situations, rather than how we would like them to be.

We have to remember who we are, what our values are, and what we are capable of. We need to consider what we want our life to look like, not just for ourselves, but for our children and loved ones. We need to be deliberate on the mindset we need to adopt, how we carry ourselves, and the steps we need to take to achieve our vision and make it a reality.

Divorce is our opportunity to be our best selves, to work for what is important to us, and to be a good role model for our kids. Some people are brought down by divorce, which is understandable, considering the weight of the emotions and pressures of the process. But by taking a different approach, and trying to make it into as positive and productive an experience as we can, we can turn a seemingly devastating situation into one that brings hope and opportunity for growth and future success.

While thinking about what got me through my divorce, and the advice I would share with others (especially those who are advocating for what they believe to be in the best interest of their child with special needs), I came up with a framework based on my greatest lessons and learnings so I could help other moms navigate the overwhelm and complexities of divorce involving a child with a disability and get the best result possible for their family.

I call my framework RISE, each letter representing key mindsets and actions to get special needs moms through divorce and work towards a successful outcome for themselves and their children. Also, doesn't the word RISE inspire you to take action, in a positive and committed fashion? It did for me. It is a call to rise above the negativity of what may be going on around you in the divorce process.

Here's a summary of the key components of RISE:

R: Recognize and Resolve

I: Identify and Investigate

S: Self-Care, Support, Secure Team, Special Needs Considerations

E: Express, Execute, Embrace

I am honored to share more about the elements of RISE, and how they can help not just divorcing moms of kids with special needs, but also any mother interested in advocating for herself and her children's needs when facing divorce. I hope you find my explanation and insights helpful as you go through your own divorce journey and consider which philosophies and approaches will work best to align with who you are and what you want out of not just the divorce, but out of life.

The R in RISE stands for Recognize and Resolve

RECOGNIZE: It is important to get in the right mindset, to confidently approach divorce and advocate for yourself and your children. We must Recognize what we are facing, accepting that divorce is happening, to take steps to achieve a successful process and outcome. Understanding that divorce is a major event in our lives, and that the loss and changes we go through mirror the phases of the Grief Cycle, can be reassuring and empowering. By learning that it is perfectly okay and natural to go through the phases of Denial, Anger, Bargaining, Depression and then Acceptance, we can be kinder and gentler to ourselves and those around us during the transition.

RESOLVE: It's important to Resolve to get the best outcome we can as part of the process. By focusing on setting and meeting goals that are important to us and our family members in divorce, we can make better decisions to help us reach our vision. Resolve takes work, and may take time, so feeling pressured or rushing into decisions that may not be in our best interest is not the way to go. The decisions we make in divorce will have a long-lasting impact, so carefully considering our actions and ramifications of choices we make in the process is very important.

The I in RISE stands for Identify and Investigate

IDENTIFY: When planning for what a child with a disability may require now and, in the future, and how much financial support would be needed, it's important to Identify what you have and what you need in terms of funds and resources in order to address your child's current and future needs. For those who have not been intimately involved or have had limited visibility and access to the finances in the household, this is the time to start gathering financial information, with the help of professionals if needed. Even for women who have been involved in the finances and investments, it is important to clearly identify all the assets and liabilities, and income and expenses, related to all members of the household.

INVESTIGATE: Raising a child with a disability can be quite re-source-intensive. It's important to Investigate the services or programs your child may need in the short and long term. We won't know what reasonable costs are and how much financial support may be needed until we take the time to research and investigate potential programs and associated costs the child may need. When a child is young, it may be difficult to predict what the child's needs and expenses may be in the future, and it may be emotionally difficult to come to terms that a child may not make the progress we are working towards, but it's a good approach to hope for the best and plan for the worst when trying to put together a future cost and funding plan.

The S in RISE stands for Self-Care, Support, Secure Team, and Special Needs Considerations

SELF-CARE: Moms of kids with disabilities tend to put their own needs and well-being last, and put all their energy into making sure everyone else's needs are addressed. But it's important to take care of YOU and engage in some form of Self-Care so you can be there for your kids, think more clearly, and make better decisions in divorce. Self-care looks different for everyone. It can be as simple as giving yourself permission for a few minutes of down time each day, to going on a vacation to decompress.

SUPPORT: We don't have to do this alone. We can seek Support from family, friends, professionals, and groups. Some divorcing women may be reluctant to ask for help, or not want to share their personal situation with others, but more often than not, others who care about us are more than willing to help and be supportive. Sometimes we need to be explicit in terms of what type of support would be most helpful to us, so others will know how they can best support us.

SECURE TEAM: It is important to find professionals who understand special needs considerations as well as eligibility for benefits to advocate for and protect your child's needs. Team members can include people with legal, financial, and mental health expertise. And, of course, working with a Divorce Coach, especially one with an understanding and experience in special needs, can help you navigate the process, be a source of ideas of things you had not considered, be a sounding board and source of emotional and logistical support, and connect you with other resources and professionals you may need on your team.

SPECIAL NEEDS CONSIDERATIONS: There are many facets of divorce involving a child with a disability that make the process and experience even more complex and challenging than a "regular" divorce. This can involve setting things up correctly so that current or future government benefits are not inadvertently jeopardized or lost. Parenting plans, possession schedules, decision making authority, child support amount and duration, supporting kids through divorce transitions, planning for the future, and addressing medical, behavioral and educational needs are just some of the factors which should be considered. They can look different when you have children with complex medical needs or intellectual or developmental disabilities.

The E in RISE stands for Express, Execute and Embrace

EXPRESS: It is important to communicate effectively with everyone involved in your divorce, from your ex to your attorney, so you can express yourself in a confident, professional manner. For example, the BIFF method, developed by Bill Eddy of the High Conflict Institute, encourages communication to be **B**rief, **I**nformative, Friendly, and **F**irm. This approach works well not just when dealing with people with high conflict personalities, but also helps those going through divorce to learn and implement skills to protect their peace and boundaries. If others see us as being calm and rational, hopefully that approach will prevail and bring things to resolution in a more efficient and productive manner. Even if the other divorcing party does not take this approach, if you communicate calmly and effectively, you are more likely to be taken seriously by your legal team, mediator, and judge, increasing the chances that things you are advocating for will go in your favor.

EXECUTE: Divorce can be overwhelming, especially with all the things that need to be considered and all steps that need to be taken to reach the finish line. But by looking at divorce actions as a project plan, breaking things down into manageable steps and taking action on your divorce goals and deadlines, you can get through the process with more focus and less stress. Don't be afraid to engage others to help as needed, to assist you in approaching divorce as a project plan to get you to your goal, rather than an emotional whirlwind without direction and vision for the future. Though it may not seem like it as you are embroiled in the thick of it, divorce is a finite process and this difficult time in your life will come to an end. With proper planning and execution, you can get there more quickly, with less stress, less expense, and hopefully a better result for you and your loved ones.

EMBRACE: Embrace the wonderful opportunities that await once divorce is complete. Divorce does not have to be seen as just an end; it is a new beginning. For example, if it were not for my divorce and the experiences I went through, I would not have the new purpose in my life and opportunities that have come my way, including writing this chapter in this book.

I sincerely hope this chapter has given you a new perspective on divorce, and how to RISE above during the challenges you may face on your journey.

These are some of the guiding principles I use as I support my coaching clients before, during, and after divorce. As I write this chapter, I am developing coaching programs around these principles so that others can learn more about these approaches and implement them in their own divorce for a more successful process and outcome.

As I reflect on what I went through and how far I have come since my divorce, I am reminded that even though we may not have envisioned or chosen the path our life has taken, we are all here for a purpose, and our life's experiences make us who we are. It is what we do with those experiences that truly defines us and how we choose to use those lessons to inspire and make a difference in the lives of others, from our own children to those who may be facing their own divorce journeys.

I often get feedback from other special needs moms and supporters thanking me for the work I do and the courage it took to take a stand for what was right for my family and to help others to do the same. But the greatest affirmation I ever received was my own son saying to me, "Mom, you're a different person now than you were before divorce.

I'm very proud of you." Isn't this what life is about, to grow and be a good role model to our kids and those around us?

What lessons and learnings will you take from your divorce to make this a better world for yourself and others?

Mary Ann Hughes

Mary Ann Hughes, MBA, mother of sons on the autism spectrum, founded Special Family Transitions after her own divorce journey, and became a Certified Special Needs Divorce Coach, Mediator, and Parenting Coordinator, to help other families save emotional energy, time, and money in their divorce transitions. Mary Ann is committed to helping families with neurodivergent or complex needs children navigate divorce and coparenting challenges in a positive and productive fashion.

Based in Houston, Texas, Mary Ann supports families across the United States and beyond, through coaching, consulting, mediation, and other services. Considered a thought leader in the field of special needs divorce, Mary Ann shares her expertise on summits, podcasts, publications, live events, and various online platforms. As the Co-Director of the Special Needs Chapter of the National Association of Divorce Professionals, as well as contributor and instructor for the CDC Certified Special Needs Coach program, Mary Ann is honored to support and educate families and professionals in divorce and transitions involving children with disabilities.

Please reach out if you feel that Mary Ann can be of assistance as you navigate your divorce challenges and help you advocate for the best result for you and your child with a disability. It would be her honor to support you.

Check out Mary Ann's resources for support at

https://www.specialfamilytransitions.com.

CHAPTER 15

From Frozen to Fired Up

Melissa K Range

I dedicate this chapter to my three precious gifts, Vivian, Luke, and Natalie. You chose me as your mother, and I am forever grateful.

If someone would have told me that within the span of 11 years I would get married, divorced, and be a single mom of three children (all by the time I was 40), I would never have believed it. When I got married, I was all in! I am the kind of woman who never gives up and who never wants to fail at anything—especially marriage.

My subconscious-mind coach has coined women like me, WIT women—women who do "whatever it takes," no matter what. After doing everything I could to save my marriage, I was out of options and unsure how to proceed. I came to a point one day when I realized I had everything I could have ever dreamed of, the nice big house, new cars,

5-star vacations, healthy, smart children, but I was miserable. I hated myself and my husband, yet no one would have known it because I put on a fabulous appearance. I had become isolated and extremely sad, angry, and solutionless as to how to fix things over the course of my marriage. Then one day, after reaching my bottom, unable to save anyone or even myself, I surrendered—something I learned in a recovery program called Al-anon—and life began to unfold in miraculous ways.

One of the biggest reasons I did not want to leave my marriage was the stigma of divorce, and also because I didn't know how to choose a lawyer or keep things private since most of his family are attorneys (his father being one of the most powerful in the Midwest). I stayed for so long frozen in fear, out of judgment of what others would say and think, and out of concern for how I would protect my assets. Looking back now, I understand my irrational logic, yet I would never recommend someone stay in a relationship where they are belittled, criticized, gaslighted, and their light is diminished. Life is too short!

After moving back into the house my ex-husband and I bought together, which never sold (and is one of many miracles in this story), I began a new life of freedom. I remember waking up the morning after I moved in, and a dove landed on the fence outside my window, signifying peace and a fresh start. I cried for hours, something I had not done in years because I had become so numb. I suffered from carpal tunnel in both wrists for many years, but within two years, the condition completely healed.

Leaving my marriage was a huge adjustment. I was pained by the fear of judgment and the breaking up of my family. Yet I knew my life was going to get better because I was on a spiritual path and was expanding daily, feeling joyful and free, away from a very toxic relationship. I had been in extreme masculine energy for a very long time as a corporate executive and sole decision maker of my family. I needed to connect to Mother Earth and my Divine Nature, a place I had forgotten existed. I did this by meditating and walking every day at a nearby park, remembering my feminine divinity.

As time went on, *reclaim your power, rebuild your intuition, and restore grace to your life* became a common theme in my life. This was a mantra I began to live by as I was grieving and healing a lifetime of low self-esteem, lack of confidence, little support, and financial fears. I did not realize the depths of pain, hurt, and abuse I had experienced because I had been in denial for so long of what I needed and wanted. I could not even form a list of what I desired in life anymore, whereas when I was younger, I was always setting goals and pursuing my dreams.

The first step of reclaiming my power began the day I left my husband. I finally made "me" a priority. It was a scary day, yet I knew it was the best decision I made for myself and my children. I took initiative, as it was a big risk, yet the payoff was huge! This set the tone for other experiences where I needed to reclaim my power and enforce what I wanted.

Six months after my divorce, I was begged by a podiatrist to work part time and I found myself in a space of being mothered, manipulated, and managed by the spa manager. She did it for months and I was exhausted from her behavior. I had been in jobs like this before and had never used my voice, so it was time to stand up! Even though I was scared to quit because the money was good and the hours were around my children's schedules, I knew I had to leave. It was another big opportunity to reclaim my power.

Making myself a priority had become high on my list of things to do. It was extremely challenging at first because I never did it before and my mother never modeled it. It's not common for women to treat themselves with acceptance, care, love, and compassion. We hear over and over again to put the oxygen mask on ourselves first then someone else, yet I think the majority of women don't listen.

With my children gone about 40% of the time, I began to invest in myself. I voraciously started to read spiritual and self-help books. I started to train with my subconscious-mind coach, a Vietnam war veteran, who was teaching people how to rewire their brains and take on a totally different perception of life. I began thinking about what I wanted and how I was going to make a difference in other people's lives. I also began to pursue my first certification in Usui Reiki. Within three months, I had become a Master Teacher, and was now able to work on clients with energy healing and teach others this magical healing work. Things I had never dreamed of were opening up within me, and reclaiming my power was in momentum. I was beginning to have fun and decided I would start my own business with my Reiki practice, even getting certified six months later in Karuna Reiki as a master teacher.

During this time of reclaiming my power, I was continually challenged by my children's father. Whether it was around demanding the children on my days for a family birthday party with no reciprocation, them having issues with no food at his house, or not getting picked up on time from school, my ex was relentless with his narcissistic behavior. There were days I would break and argue with him, justifying my reactive and emotionally charged behavior, and other times that I would say nothing and cry alone. There were periods when I had to call my Al-anon sponsor daily to vent and be heard, which was a life saver. There was definitely lots of growth to be had! I knew my ego had put me into all this fear, and I was determined to find my authentic self.

After divorcing my husband relatively quickly, with no alimony and only minimal child support, I was overwhelmed by the fear of financial insecurity. This was an entirely new reality for me, as I had been working consistently since the age of 11 and had managed to build substantial savings. However, I found myself forced to dip into my 401(k) to make ends meet. I began to delve into my relationship with money and started reading books related to all of the layers of shame, lack, and scarcity I believed in regarding money. This is not an easy topic to discuss, especially for women and most definitely because we give most of the power of our finances to men. Did you know that back in matriarchal systems, women held the keys to the banks? I found this out in my two-year Crystalline Priestess certification. I also delved deep into my shadow regarding money and with my subconscious-mind coach I began to do scientifically written affirmations to help build a new brain, one that only sees abundance and prosperity.

One of the main things I began to perceive as well was all the miracles occurring in my life! Since I had opened up my intuition and was learning to fine tune it and follow it, I saw how life was supporting me. Did you know that your intuition is one of your superpowers? It's your inner guidance or personal GPS. I cannot stress enough the value of learning to awaken and hone your intuition.

I remember one day, a few months after leaving my husband, I was beginning to feel that scarcity emotion around money. Then my father told my sisters and me he was gifting us each $13,000 just because! The relief this caused in my body and mind was tremendous. It was another time when I had let Spirit take the lead, meaning I turned it over and trusted everything to work out exquisitely better than I could have ever planned. I was beginning to trust myself and saw when I let go, life could flow. At the time, I didn't realize it, but I was transitioning away from the masculine energy that had dominated my life for so long and embracing my feminine energy, which became a protective cocoon for me for many years. I had been out of balance for so long, the pendulum swung to the extreme, and it took me many years to bring it back to where I now know how to utilize both energies when I need them.

The journey of loving myself and being my own boss continued as I moved my Reiki and coaching practice into a leased space owned by a friend from my spiritual book club. I needed to experience this relationship with her in order to understand the importance of boundaries and how even though someone seems spiritual and all "love and light," if they haven't done the deep inner work, or continue to spiritually bypass, you have to let go and realize you are your own guru! I faced this in a big way and was extremely frustrated, yet I knew after seven months in this space I was being mothered, manipulated and managed again, and I chose to create some strict boundaries until my one-year lease was up. This led me to work from home, once again patiently waiting for Spirit to lead me to the next level.

I got this next lead in 2017, which was a huge year of growth for me! I woke up in January and heard, "Melissa, it's time for you to go firewalking." This idea had been rolling around in my head for years, implanted in my mind by my subconscious-mind coach, who did this with previous clients to get them to walk through their fear. I did some research and, within three weeks of hearing the call, I drove 600 miles alone to Texas, walked on 12 feet of broken glass, broke boards and bricks with my bare hands, and walked on 1400-degree coals over 110 times. It pushed my ego to the limit, and I literally transformed my inner being in four days' time. There is nothing like doing extreme spiritual activities such as these to blow us open to our unlimited potential! I was on a high for days after this and felt unstoppable.

When I returned home, my intuition was even more honed because I had listened and taken action. When we act on what we hear intuitively, we create trust and faith in ourselves and in what I call Spirit. Not only that, I had been recruited to teach ballroom dance after only taking two lessons myself, and the dance was opening up my shakti or womb space, and I was remembering a deeper part of my Divine Feminine

Nature. This led me to hear another intuitive call, and in March of that year I enrolled in an Akashic Record Reading certification, where I came to find out I had mediumship abilities. I didn't believe it at first, yet once I began to trust what I was hearing during readings, I was blown open again to helping others who wanted to connect with someone on the other side. People were coming out of the woodwork to get readings with me, and I was on a new path of growth!

In 2017, I was invited to join Priestess school, and I accepted, even though it was a two-year commitment and a huge financial investment. I was very nervous because I did not know what to expect, yet I heard the call and heeded it. Listening and acting on what you hear builds confidence. One of the reasons so many people stay stuck in their lives is because they sit there and do nothing. Doing nothing is an action, by the way, yet where does it get you? Nowhere! And when nothing changes, nothing changes. I tell others all the time that I do not like to sit in fear, and I would rather walk through the fear and anxiety than sit in it or regret not going after what I want.

This two-year program would prove to be one of the most challenging and most redemptive of my life! I am so grateful I took the leap, because it pushed me into remembering the Goddess I am. Without this training, I would never have known how revered the Goddess is, and this transformation radiates not only to my own daughters, but to everyone in the world. I remembered at the deepest core of myself my value and worth as a woman. This has been oppressed in all women for thousands of years because men fear our power.

In early 2018, my mother was diagnosed with lung cancer, and then brain cancer. My parents needed assistance, and I was the only daughter that could work it into her schedule. I began to spend a lot of time with my parents. This was extremely important, because it meant an opportunity to heal all the karmic lessons I had with them, plus those in my forward and backward lineage. I had a strong foundation rooted in Al-Anon, Adult Children of Alcoholics, and my priestess circle. My self-care practice was well-established, and I shared a beautiful, loving connection with Spirit, who had been restoring grace to my life for years. I felt confident and positive I could face anything. I was also coaching many clients by this time, and I had received another certification as a Money Breakthrough Business Coach and Sacred Money Archetypes coach.

A little less than two years later, my father became ill and died within five days. We had to move our mom to assisted living, then the pandemic hit, we got a puppy, and my children were here 24/7 on Zoom calls for school in our tiny house. My mother died nine months after my dad, and then my mentor died. I was at my breaking point. I went down into the depths of my own personal hell where I stayed for two-and-a-half years. I felt alone, trapped, and abandoned. I was experiencing another dark night of the soul. I was frozen in fear and I wondered how I would ever get out!

A friend asked me recently, "Melissa, how did you get out of that space?" I went on to share with her that it was a decision to make a change. I realized I was living in constant fear, and I had done that rodeo before and couldn't stay there. The grief of so much loss was overwhelming, yet my heart needed some hope. I saw the duality of life at its fullest, yet my greatest power in that moment was choice. I chose me, and I chose love. Every day I get to choose what to believe, how to live, who I'm in relationship with at any given moment. I stopped believing someone or something was going to save me. I remembered I can say no or yes when it feels right, based on my intuition, and I let go of hierarchies and began to trust only myself and my Creator.

Last summer, I finally was ready to get back to serving others with my work, since I had stopped seeing clients in June of 2022. My oldest two children had gone off to college and only my youngest is at home now. I joined a mastermind and learned how to create a 5-week program for women called "Find Your Fire." My dream is for women to remember their inherent Divine Nature and their feminine power. Women have gotten so far away from chasing our dreams and desires, it makes me sad. And in the past few years, our rights have been challenged, which really burns me up!

I would love to remind you of three steps you can take right away as you move forward in your life after divorce.

First, make yourself a priority. Do something every day that feeds you, such as exercise, art, music, a manicure or bubble bath.

Second, learn to hone your intuition. This is done through meditation, alone time in nature, singing bowls, transformational breathwork, or energy work.

Third, get into action with what you truly want from life. Make a list of your dreams and desires and then take baby steps to get there.

If I did it, so can you! You are powerful and you deserve to be the Whole woman you were meant to be.

Melissa K Range

Melissa K Range is a single mom of three certified lifeguards who have saved over 20 lives combined, plus Apollo the friendliest dog in town. Melissa loves to travel (especially if it means playing with fire), meet new people, and live interdependently by her own lights. Tell her she can't do something, and she will probably reply, "Watch me!"

After graduating from college, she began her career in corporate America utilizing her fluency in Spanish. Soon thereafter, she was recruited by a pharmaceutical company where she was awarded Rookie of the year and President's Club for top sales.

She has been on a spiritual path for 15 years, being inspired to evolve through multiple certifications such as Firewalk instructor, Crystalline Priestess, Money Breakthrough Business coach, Sacred Money Archetypes coach, and Doula. She's also an Usui, Karuna, Angelic, and Crystal Reiki Master Teacher, Akashic record reader, and former Zumba and ballroom dance instructor.

Melissa mentors and empowers women to rebuild their intuition, reclaim their power, and restore grace to their lives by reminding them of who they are, and helping them to push their edge through focused action to create what they want in life. She is a staunch believer in the fierce feminine and has adopted the term WIT—whatever it takes—for women who are willing to own their shadow and lead with their heart.

Connect with Melissa at https://findyourfire.my.canva.site/.

CHAPTER 16

Out of the Deepest Darkness Emerges the Most Brilliant Light

Myriam-Rose Kohn

To my parents, Alexander Kohn and Flora Schachnovitz,
who by example instilled in me gratitude, integrity, and the
fortitude to survive.

I was raised the old-fashioned way, which means I was raised to be a good, dutiful wife who did everything for her husband. All the meals were always cooked from scratch with the healthiest ingredients and I learned how to sew, which led to my husband wearing tailor-made clothes. So imagine—after thinking I was the perfect wife—my surprise when one Monday night my husband came home at 5 p.m. and informed me he was leaving the next morning at 9 a.m. ostensibly for a trial separation.

Well, if it were a trial separation, why was he taking all his clothes with him as well as some household goods? Unbeknownst to me, he had bought a condo two miles down the street. How he was able to do this without my consent, I will never know.

All the while we were married, I would hear any variation of how stupid, how illogical, how incompetent, how incapable of doing anything right I was. That was piled on top of having heard ever since I was five years old that I would never amount to anything. But then I thought, if he were right, why was I the one doing everything? And trouble started because in order not to yell, I started to drink. How I never became an alcoholic is a mystery to me, but a good one. Today I never have the need for a drink. I hardly touch alcohol at all.

Back to the family situation. Clearly, the handwriting was on the wall. He never allowed me to work while we were married because that would have meant he was not a "good provider." So when he left, I had no savings, no money in the bank, no resources for anything. How was I going to pay the mortgage, feed our children, and provide for anything else necessary?

Those were dark days. My heart was constantly beating out of my chest. Whereas I used to pride myself on my memory, now I couldn't remember anything from one moment to another. I cried every day whenever I was alone. I honestly don't know how I got through that time. It was just one day at a time. Even now, however, that five-year period is a black hole to me. I cannot remember anything that happened during those first five years after he left. It's like a self-protecting wall is still in place. I have definitely moved on, though.

I am getting ahead of myself so let's backtrack. While we were married, we never made friends as a couple. I had made a couple of friends on my own, but my husband completely alienated them. I certainly could not call my parents for help, as they were still living in Belgium. They did not have the financial means to help me and I did not want to hear that I was a failure as a wife.

So I had no one to turn to. There was no such thing as a career coach back in those days. What was I going to do? No stranger to hard work (I had self-financed my college education by working 52 hours a week and carrying 16 units a semester, going sometimes two to three months without having a single day off, and yet graduated with honors), I found a part-time job as an instructor of French a couple of years before he left. As you may suspect, my husband did everything he could to sabotage everything I tried. For the teaching which took place in the evenings, he was conveniently not home because he had other commitments (which he never had before) so I put the children in the back of the classroom.

Fortunately, I was not penalized for this unprofessionalism. I requested a couple more classes. Besides French, I taught sewing. This was my first transition: from housewife to part-time teacher. Eventually, I found work as an adjunct instructor at the local junior college and also at the state university where I taught French (I hold a Master of Arts in French and a Bachelor of Arts in French and German with a minor in Italian). I also taught some German and Italian at the junior college.

It was a lot of work and all I seemed to do was work, take care of the children, and take them to their various seasonal activities such as baseball, basketball, soccer, gymnastics, dance…. You know the routine.

In the meantime, I decided to put my language skills to good use and took a test to become an accredited translator. That examination was very tough. Only 29% of all applicants succeed and I succeeded on my first try, which reinforced my belief in my abilities, thereby discrediting decades of being told I would never amount to anything.

The next step was to apply to become state certified. This exam was divided into one part written and one part oral. Again, I had success on the first try! Now I could be listed in the database of the Administrative Courts for the Judicial Council of the State of California. This made me visible to attorneys and other courts throughout the State of California. They could call me for translation work, and once in a while I would be called upon to go and interpret in a court.

This certification required continuing education. In between juggling that, teaching, and my business, I still took care of my children. The need to be there for them was very strong. I am a nurturer, no two ways about it.

After two years of this, my ex came back for the children. He dragged out the divorce for three years so that he would not have to pay child support. He never paid spousal support, either.

With me, our sons had responsibilities and my resources were limited. With him, they had no responsibilities and he gave them whatever they wanted. The children (I should say teens) quickly figured out how to manipulate him.

In the beginning, our children were to be two weeks with me and two weeks with him. The upheaval every two weeks was just too hard on them. So we tried three weeks and then four. It just tore me apart to see them struggling with the move every time. I offered them to stay wherever they chose, hoping in my heart—but knowing better in my head—that they would choose fewer resources with a family rather than the other option. Being growing men, they naturally chose their father.

The result was that I felt like I had failed as a mother as well; however, I just could not live with myself seeing the pain my sons were going through every time they had to move. My conscience is clear and this does not keep me up at night anymore. I feel I made the right decision.

It took me nine years to put myself back together again. During that time, laughter was a distant memory. The crying gradually came to a stop. After all, what was the use?

One evening I was watching a show with an extremely funny comedian. I started to laugh and it actually hurt. It physically hurt. I hadn't laughed in such a long time that I had actually forgotten what it was like. I remember that moment so clearly as if it were yesterday. It took a few more episodes of watching comedy or listening to comedians before it stopped hurting to laugh.

When I emerged on the other side of those nine years, I was no longer the same woman. Gone was the dutiful wife. Oh, I still cook from scratch because I like to know what is in my food, but my attitude had changed. First of all, for the first time in my life, I saw myself as a valuable human being, one who believed in herself. At the urging of my sons—they must have known something I didn't—I took back my maiden name. That one move empowered me. Although changed, I was myself again. Well, a new me.

In addition to the part-time teaching, I started a business where I provided administrative support services in 19 languages. My clients started asking me to prepare resumes for them. Always trying to do the best for my clients, I investigated what resumes entailed. I found the Professional Association for Resume Writers (at that time it was the only organization; today, there are four of them), studied, took the examination and became a Certified Professional Resume Writer.

Your resume only gets your foot in the door; your interview gets you the position. I wanted to be able to provide more value for my clients and not just prepare their resume, but help them land the positions they were seeking, so I studied to become a Certified Employment Interview Professional and passed.

You may have noticed I use the word position instead of job. I don't like the word job because it implies you have to do something you don't want to do. When you say the word "job," it's like saying, "I have to get up in the morning and go to work" rather than looking forward to your day and discovering surprises life has in store for you.

Now my clients are in their new position and they are encountering all kinds of unexpected hurdles. To keep things short, I became a Certified Career Management Coach and eventually a Master Career Director so I could coach my clients with anything they needed career-wise.

As you can see, I am transitioning into having a full-time business with all things career. I am still accepting translation work so that I'm covered in case I do not have enough work in my business.

When I was married, I never imagined I could or would be doing what I'm doing today. It's been an exciting journey, one that started against my will. Sometimes we need to be pushed out of the nest in order to fly. That's exactly what's happened for me.

I will continue to grow and learn no matter how old I get. In addition to all of the other trainings and certifications I've attained, I was among the first 50 worldwide Certified Personal Brand Strategists. In my training, there were colleagues from China, Singapore, South Africa, England, and France. I became a Certified Digital Brand Strategist, as well as a Certified Job Search Strategist.

Education is a leitmotif in my life. My ex used to laugh at me and asked if I was going to be a perpetual student. Thank goodness I am, especially in today's world. My children are adults now, but I still have the need to educate and to nurture.

Enter my clients. While I have a difficult time attracting new clients, once I succeed, our relationship lasts way beyond the time we work together. They become lifelong clients. The world changes for them, too, so they need guidance in this new employment market. Many of them have also sent their children to me for their career needs.

I started attending conferences in the mid-'90s and that allowed me to meet with book and newspaper publishers. To date, my work has appeared in more than 35 books. One particular newspaper editor attended one of these conferences and urged me to write an article about international resumes. He was the editor of The National Business Employment Weekly, currently renamed CareerJournal.com, the business edition of The Wall Street Journal. Never in my wildest dreams would I have thought to write or even submit an article to them. The editor gave me style guidelines to which I adhered. He published my article and gave me a page and a half spread in the paper. That was back in the days when the paper was still printed.

This event really boosted my confidence. The exposure brought me several financial executives as clients who also recommended me to their friends, furthering my belief in my abilities.

One thing I had always dreamt of doing was being a speaker on stage. I have no idea why. Being in front of a classroom is not the same thing.

After attending a few conferences during which the event planners got to know me, I eventually was offered to speak. I have addressed conferences with 500+ attendees in the room; however, I wanted to hone my speaking abilities. I needed to learn how to introduce humor in the right place and how to hold my body for maximum effect, so I embarked on two year-long courses. That led me to start a podcast. Like all beginnings, it is small. So far, I've had only a few wonderful guests, but now that I have faith, I know it will grow. You can find my podcast, Living A Joyous & Harmonious Life Podcast where you listen to podcasts.

In 2012, my business had become viable, with a growing pipeline of clients. However, tragedy struck when I lost my father, forcing me to fly back to Belgium to arrange his funeral and care for my mother, who was already in a convalescent home due to Alzheimer's and Parkinson's. Juggling my responsibilities in both countries, including working with a notary and managing administrative tasks, proved overwhelming. Without support from my brother and unable to maintain my business pipeline, my business eventually collapsed. Despite regularly flying back to Belgium to manage my mother's care, her passing and the onset of COVID further upended my life.

During the pandemic, I took the opportunity to rebuild my business, focusing on systems that made it more efficient. While I continue to help people who want to increase their salary within their current fields, I've found my true calling in guiding career transitions. I realized that many people stay in jobs that make them miserable, fearing the loss of financial stability. This unhappiness often seeps into their personal lives, leading to strained relationships. Today, I ensure my clients get paid for work they enjoy, empowering them to live more fulfilling lives. The employment landscape has drastically changed since COVID, and with so many future roles yet to be created, flexibility and imagination are key to thriving in this new world.

If you do what you love, you will have fewer headaches and lower blood pressure which in turns means fewer diseases. You go home happier and you have a better quality of life.

A toxic environment plays an important part in all of this as well. Five years ago, I stopped teaching. I love to teach, but between the kind of students who started to attend (not showing up at least a third of a semester, not doing the required work, the lack of respect) and the pressure of the administration to fill out student learning outcomes, the pressure became unbearable. After I stopped teaching, within two months, without any medication whatsoever, my blood pressure dropped from 173 to 119.

Putting all these experiences together: the career transitions, the fears, the doubts, I am well equipped to assist my clients through their transition. I have lived through it. I help my clients avoid all of this by staying by their side. They have someone to turn to when they have a question or if they need a sounding board. I have their best interests at heart. It is what separates me from the resume and coaching mills out there.

Nothing gives me greater satisfaction today than seeing my clients' faces bloom once they begin to see the new possibilities and realize they have a new lease on life.

I went from insignificant housewife to a business owner whose work has been published in 35+ books and whose article was published in CareerJournal.com (business section of The Wall Street Journal), and I still keep growing. No one will ever put me down again. It took a strong belief in myself and knowing I was on the right path which gave me the strength to start over again.

I am never letting anyone tell me again that I'm not worthwhile. My former sister-in-law, with whom I'm still good friends, told me that my ex told her he had made a mistake. Too bad. I am a lot stronger than I used to be and actually it is thanks to him. If he had not left, I would never have become what I am today. And I have not finished yet. So it's true what they say: Every cloud really does have a silver lining.

Myriam-Rose Kohn

Myriam-Rose Kohn is a multilingual career expert who had to go through two career transitions herself. In her program, she doesn't just do textbook theories. She brings real life experiences. She knows where the pitfalls and the fear lie. That's why she holds her clients' hands until they reach their goal. They do not have to do it alone. In her, they have a confidante who has their best interest at heart. Her vision is to ensure her clients get paid for work they enjoy doing so they can lead a harmonious and joyous life.

Her process consists of career exploration; resume, LinkedIn profile writings; how to ace interviews and salary negotiations; how to conduct a job search; personal and digital branding. Her work has been published in 35+ books and CareerJournal.com. She has spoken at conferences in the U.S. and Canada. Her clients are in the U.S., Europe, and Asia.

She was an adjunct professor at the university for more than 20 years. She is an accredited translator (for international clients) who also works for the courts and the U.S. Department of Justice.

Her target audience consists of people who are unhappy at work, burned out, unemployed, having to return to work after some time off; executives who want to downsize, military people returning to civilian life, and people looking for a salary increase.

Connect with Myriam-Rose at

https://reimagineyourcareernow.com.

CHAPTER 17

Discovering the GIFTS in Your Divorce by Recognizing Pivotal Life Lessons!

Rosalind Sedacca, CDC

Lovingly dedicated to my son, Cass, who continues to be the light of my life, and a daily source of love and support in all that I do.

I've faced many difficult moments in my life. But preparing to tell my 11-year-old son that I will be divorcing his father was one of the worst.

I struggled with anxiety for weeks. When should we tell him? What should we say? How do you tell a child that the life he has known is about to be disrupted—forever? How do you tell him that it's not his fault? And how do you prepare him for all the unknowns looming ahead when you're not sure how it will turn out?

My greatest concerns were: How do I …

> *break the news without breaking my son's heart?*

> *work out the custody details without chaos and confusion?*

> *communicate with my son's father without generating mistrust and resentfulness?*

> *co-parent effectively and successfully without destroying my child's life?*

> *move on, post-divorce, without leaving a legacy of pain, sorrow and anger?*

I made it my mission to remember we are, and always will be, a family, which means treating each other with compassion, empathy and respect. It wasn't easy. We made many mistakes. But step by step we figured it out and made it work. Primarily by talking. And listening attentively to my son. We put ourselves in his shoes when making decisions. We tried to cooperate, often apologized, revised our plans, learned to be flexible, and yes, forgiving!

One day, more than a decade later, my son came to visit me. He was in his early 20s. Out of the blue, he thanked me for the way his dad and I handled the divorce and especially our co-parenting. He told me most of his friends whose parents divorced were either angry or quite resentful toward them. He mentioned how close he feels to me and his father and acknowledged us for doing a great job as co-parents!

That was one of the signature moments in my life. I let out a deep sigh of relief, releasing much of the guilt I had been holding onto for years. It felt so good to know my son didn't hate me about the divorce. In fact, he still loved both his dad and me and said he had a wonderful childhood, despite the divorce. What more could a parent want?

My adult son is now happily married and gave me the joy of becoming a grandmother! There's no greater gift than seeing your child thriving in life. He's still quite close to his father and me — and I am eternally grateful!

In fact, that experience became the catalyst for my founding the Child-Centered Divorce Network. I became a Certified Divorce & Co-Parenting Coach, a podcast host and wrote numerous books, e-courses and programs on many facets of divorce, co-parenting, and dating after divorce when you have children.

In this chapter, I am sharing some of the insights I uncovered through my own experiences as well as working with my coaching clients for close to 20 years! I call them Life Lessons because they became the foundation for creating a positive and rewarding post-divorce life!

LIFE LESSON 1: Find the Gifts in Your Divorce!

When we are in the midst of life trauma, it is very difficult to focus on anything but the pain, disappointment and hurt related to that experience. That's only natural. But very often, looking back in hindsight, we can find meaning, relevance, valuable lessons and insights that were the direct result of those major life challenges.

Without that life-altering event, we would not become the people we are today.

I look upon that result as the gift I received from the experience. It became the turning point I needed to move on to a new chapter in my life. I can look back and say, while the lessons were tough, I don't regret them. In fact, I am grateful.

For behind most every tough lesson I found a great reward. I believe you can too! Are there outcomes you can be thankful for?

The greatest lesson in self-awareness comes from finding the value in key life experiences. So start by asking yourself some important questions:

What went wrong in my love relationship – and why?

What part did I play in the break-up of my marriage?

If I had responded earlier to red flag warnings, might I have changed the outcome, reduced the pain, put us back on track or better protected me and the kids?

These are hard questions to answer. It can be helpful to find a therapist, coach or support group to guide you in finding meaningful insights. Be careful that you don't get stuck on your regrets. Look for the gift. Find the lessons you can learn now. They will become the catalyst to help you move ahead with more confidence in creating a happier future.

Here are some additional questions to consider:

What did you learn as a result of your divorce experience?

Who are you today that you would not have been had you not divorced?

Do you see inner wisdom or strength that makes you proud?

Have you made decisions that are more supportive of your life and values?

Do you like yourself better?

Have you found new career directions or new meaning in life as a direct result of your divorce?

If you can't yet see positive answers to any of these questions, give yourself time. Perhaps you have not fully moved through the inner and outer transitions resulting from your divorce. Perhaps you are still holding on to resentment, anger, jealousy or other negative emotions that are keeping you from experiencing the freedom from old programming and patterns.

I believe there is a gift in every tough experience in our lives if we choose to see it. And why shouldn't we put our energy in that direction? What good does it do to hold on to a past that has slipped away? Or to people who don't give us the love and support we deserve?

When we let go of the past, we open the door to a new future. Only then can we empower ourselves to create a much better outcome for ourselves and those we love.

It's the old adage: Every cloud has a silver lining. It is true. Search for the gifts related to your divorce and it becomes yet another step toward a successful recovery from the trauma of that experience.

Of course, that takes looking within. The reward of a beautiful flower is dependent upon the internal intelligence of the seed and the root system. It is the same with humans. Do the inner work and you see the outer rewards.

Don't be afraid to go within and plant the seeds for the tomorrow you dream about. With love and patience, your garden will flourish!

LIFE LESSON 2: It's Up to You to Transform Your Life!

Divorce is always a life-altering experience. But it doesn't have to be all negative. For many, including me, it became a time of personal self-discovery. For others, it can manifest as a self-made prison of depression and resentment.

What makes the difference? I believe it's our acceptance of what is and our ability to use the divorce as a steppingstone to a new and better life.

The bottom line: it's all up to us.

We can generate an attitude of positive expectation or we can choose instead a life filled with the pain of self-pity and despair.

The real challenge: changing our attitude or perspective on life is not a simple task. But if you take consistent steps in that direction, you'll create the foundation for a happier future — both for yourself and the children you love.

Start by focusing your attention on these 3 key points to transforming your life in the months and years ahead. You'll never regret it.

1. Boost your self-esteem and self-confidence.

Don't let divorce take its toll on your self-esteem, especially if you didn't choose the breakup of your marriage. Feeling rejected, abused or like a helpless victim undermines how you view yourself and your value to others. A fear-based mindset can keep you from moving on after divorce to a new and more rewarding reality.

No one can take your pride and confidence from you. You must decide for yourself that you're ready to create a better life by seeking out and embracing the possibilities ahead. Choose to make proactive decisions, look for new supportive friends, engage your energy in fulfilling activities. Are there parts of you that were dormant during your marriage? Now's the time to tap into those attributes or interests and let them soar. Your children will benefit from watching you re-discover who you are. Better still, they'll see you as a positive role model as you tackle life's challenges.

2. *Experience the blessings that come with forgiveness.*

Forgiveness is not for or about the other person. It releases you from the pain of staying bound up in the past. Blaming yourself or your former spouse does nothing toward improving your life. Instead, it keeps you from really enjoying today — as well as tomorrow. Understanding the gift of forgiveness is a huge step forward. It may require reaching out for professional help in letting go, moving on and understanding the incredible value of forgiveness as a positive tool for self-empowerment. Remember, forgiveness doesn't mean condoning the pain you experienced in the past; it means you're not letting it hurt you anymore! Forgiving your former spouse is about breaking the emotional bonds that have held you hostage to old hurts and memories. It frees you to make healthy new connections — and that's the path to creating happier tomorrows!

Part of the forgiveness process involves letting go of the past. Living in the past is usually painful. It's filled with disappointments and regrets, neither of which support us. The past is also full of old baggage ready to be discarded. Too many of us carry that baggage with us into new relationships, not understanding the damage it does to that relationship. When we forgive ourselves and forgive those who hurt us, we cut the cord that connects us to past pain.

Forgiveness is the greatest gift we can give ourselves.

It doesn't mean we forget the wrongs. It means we stop letting them hurt and re-wound us over and over again!

3. *Revise your expectations about healthy relationships.*

What have you learned about relationship success? Did you originally choose the right marriage partner? Or had you accepted or settled for less than you imagined? Did you have unrealistic expectations about the challenges involved in a committed relationship? Do you now have different requirements for a love partner in terms of interests, values or goals?

Successful relationships require real skills in communicating, resolving conflict, and coping with a multitude of other issues. It's even more complicated when children are involved. Before stepping out into the singles-dating arena, do your homework. Learn about who you really are, what you can give, and what you need in return to create a fulfilling intimate relationship that works. Give yourself the time. Get the professional support you may need. Do it right — for you and your children! Your future lies ahead. Make it one you desire — and deserve!

LIFE LESSON 3: Take Steps Toward Rebuilding Your Self-Esteem

Authentic self-esteem comes from self-love. We truly cannot love others if we cannot find a way to first love ourselves. Life is an INSIDE job. We have to look within, clean up from within and find value within ourselves before we can ever see that light in someone else. And when we do, it will shine brighter!

Here are 5 tips for boosting your self-esteem while strengthening your self-love.

1. *Be mindful of what you expect and accept!*

We teach people how to treat us. If we accept abuse, tolerate ridicule, lack compassion for others, are overly critical, filled with anger, mistreat others or accept mistreatment, we are setting ourselves up for painful relationships both personally and professionally. With improved self-esteem, self-love and self-understanding we become more tolerant of ourselves. That leads to greater tolerance of others, a quality that deepens our relationships and attracts more love to us.

2. *Strive for peace over drama!*

I used to live a life filled with drama regarding my relationship ups and downs. Fighting and making up, crying and looking for the next exciting event — it took its toll on my life. Now I strive for PEACE. I don't need excitement or drama to be happy. I find joy in nature, doing what I love, talking with close friends and family, spending time with myself. It makes for a much happier and more fulfilling life.

3. *Catch your self-talk!*

We are often our own worst enemy without being aware of it. When we listen to our self-talk, we can catch ourselves being overly critical, hurtful and disrespectful to who we are! We can then self-correct. We'd never talk to another person the way we too often ridicule ourselves with little compassion. Change your self-talk and you can change the outcome of your life. Catch yourself doing things right and give yourself a hug. We don't have to wait for others to acknowledge us or provide the support we need!

4. *Stop comparing yourself with others!*

Social media has heightened our ability to compare every facet of our lives with friends and strangers. That becomes a great excuse to put yourself down or feel less valuable than others in your universe. Stop the madness. You are a unique YOU and not supposed to be a version of someone else. Let go of ridiculous comparisons with those who are wealthier, younger, smarter, thinner, more talented or successful. Be proud of who you are and what you bring to this world. Focus on that and your life will be more satisfying and fulfilling than you ever imagined!

5.   *Take responsibility for the part you played.*

It's easy to feel like a victim in your divorce and put all the blame on your former spouse. But that keeps you stuck in a place without growth. Before you can move beyond your divorce you have to "own" the role you played in the marriage as well as the insights you can use in the months ahead. When we take responsibility for experiences in our lives, we have the power to make positive changes—and that's essential for creating the brighter future we all desire and deserve.

LIFE LESSON 4: Accept Your New Reality with Positive Expectations

Accepting the reality and finality of divorce can be a tough challenge. We need to be able to let go of the life we knew and prepare to face an unknown future. That can be intimidating. Here are 3 key steps to accepting your new reality with grace, peace and positive expectations for a happier life ahead, especially if you're also a parent!

1.   *Focus on yourself—not on your former spouse*

We can't ever undo the past, but the past can undo us—if we're not careful about our thoughts, beliefs and actions.

The only one we can ever change is ourselves. Don't waste valuable time pining about the past, blaming your ex or wishing you had done something differently. Focus instead on how you can transform yourself today into the person you most want to be. When you shift from within, things on the outside will shift as well. Only then can you choose to make healthier decisions about your life and your future life partner.

2.   *Seek out the support you need*

Tough times demand support systems if we want to progress into the next stage in our lives. Recovering from the wounds of divorce is not something to tackle alone. Reach out for a coach, therapist, support group or member of the clergy experienced in this work. It will accelerate your progress while boosting your self-esteem. There is no shame in needing support. The world's top athletes, entrepreneurs, actors and others all depend on coaches to achieve greater success!

3. *Remember, you are a role model for your children*

Regardless of whether they acknowledge it or not, your children are watching and learning from you through lessons both good and bad. What are you teaching them about how to recover from a challenge in life? What are they learning about how to deal with conflict and difficult people around you? What lessons are they getting about taking responsibility for your life and your actions? What are you modeling about being a victim versus becoming victorious, despite tough times? Your children will thank you for being a mature, responsible parent and showing them how to overcome challenging situations. Step up and BE the parent they need now and in the future!

Be gentle with yourself as you flow through the process.

Don't judge or get angry with yourself for feeling depressed, embarrassed, hurt or other emotions. It's a natural part of the grieving and moving on process after divorce. Accept your feelings and keep looking for the lessons you've learned through your marriage and divorce. They become the gifts that support you when you're ready to step out into your new reality. If you're feeling stuck in any emotion and can't let go, reach out for the help you need from an experienced professional. Remember, you're not alone, so don't isolate yourself or stay immersed in your pain.

***Be sure to <u>grab my complimentary ebook</u> on Post-Divorce Parenting Success Strategies to guide you in creating a rewarding Child-Centered Divorce for your own family* here:**

<u>www.childcentereddivorce.com/book</u>

Rosalind Sedacca, CDC

Rosalind Sedacca, CDC, is recognized as The Voice of Child-Centered Divorce. She is a Certified Divorce & Co-Parenting Coach, founder and director of the Child-Centered Divorce Network. Working nationally and internationally, she provides support, coaching, online programs and other valuable resources for parents who are facing, moving through, or transitioning beyond their divorce.

Rosalind is a divorced parent herself. She understands the anxiety, guilt, anger, fear, frustration and pain parents experience during and after divorce. She is the author of *How Do I Tell the Kids About the Divorce? A Create-a-Storybook Guide to Preparing Your Children – With Love!* — an internationally acclaimed ebook designed to help parents get through the tough divorce talk with the best possible outcome for themselves and their children. Rosalind has also created several ebooks and e-courses on co-parenting success strategies including an 8-hour Anger Management For Co-Parents course.

She shares profound wisdom on attracting healthy new relationships post-divorce, while always being mindful about your children.

In addition, she also hosts the Divorce, Dating & Empowered Living Radio Show & Podcast.

Rosalind's primary concern is guiding her clients toward minimizing any negative effects on their children — not only in the months ahead, but in the decades to follow, as well.

Learn more about Rosalind's services and resources at

https://www.childcentereddivorce.com.

CHAPTER 18

From Surviving to Thriving

Stacy McAlpine

When I sat down to write this chapter, I thought about all the moments that brought me here—moments I could barely get through at the time, let alone imagine sharing with anyone. And how far I've come since then, on the other side, and able to share lessons I learned from my journey to help others.

Where do I even begin?

Do I start with the years I spent trying to hold everything together?

The betrayals I discovered and endured for the sake of my kids?

The nights I cried myself to sleep, wondering if I'd ever find the strength to leave?

Or maybe I should start on the other side of it all.

The moment I had my freedom again.

The pride I felt when I realized I'd broken a generational pattern of emotional abuse.

The joy of waking up every morning to a life I truly love.

After sitting with all these questions, I realized this chapter isn't about any one moment. It's about the journey. The choices I made—some terrifying, some liberating—that brought me here. And, most importantly, the lessons I learned along the way and can now share with you.

Before

My story didn't start with my former husband. It started long before, with a childhood shaped by a narcissistic father. At the time, I didn't realize what narcissism was or how deeply it influenced me.

I grew up learning to adapt to emotional manipulation, to put others' needs above my own, and to suppress what mattered most to me.

When I married my former husband, I unknowingly walked right back into a familiar pattern of manipulation and emotional abuse. It felt normal—until it didn't.

It took me seven years of therapy (and a lot of tissues) to finally see the reality of my situation. My therapist never gave up on me, even when I wanted to give up on myself (thank you, Deborah!).

She showed me the tactics my husband at the time was using to keep me in line and how blind I had been to them.

She helped me see that it didn't have to be that way.

But what got me to act didn't happen in my therapist's office —it was a very specific moment that I will always remember.

My Wake-Up Call

My oldest daughter, seven years old at the time, had a friend over to play. I overheard her apologizing for something she hadn't even done. She was bending over backward to make her friend happy, accepting the manipulation as though it were normal.

It hit me right in the heart strings.

I saw myself in her. Every apology I had made just to keep the peace. Every time I had let someone else's happiness take precedence over my own. When my daughter was in the back seat and whispered, *"I love you mommy,"* as she witnessed husband at the time berating me. And how I immediately tensed up worrying that her saying that would make him even madder

I remember thinking, *Oh my God, she's becoming me.* And I recognized that not wanting your own kids to be like you was a red flag I couldn't ignore.

The reality was that I was modeling behaviors that would shape my daughters' beliefs about themselves, their worth, and what is okay to tolerate. I couldn't let them grow up thinking this was what love looked like.

I had spent years convincing myself that staying in my marriage was the "right" thing to do for my girls. But in that moment, I realized that staying wasn't protecting my daughters—it was teaching them to accept the unacceptable

I thought I was just being "strong" by tolerating emotional manipulation, but all I was doing was repeating history. And worst of all, I was passing it on to my own daughters. That realization was the wake-up call that changed everything.

My youngest, who was just three at the time, hadn't yet started mimicking the patterns outright, but I knew she was watching, learning what relationships and love were supposed to look like.

I felt a deep urgency to act before this pattern had the chance to take hold of her, too. And for my oldest, it was a race against time. I could already see the behaviors taking root, and the thought of her carrying them into her own relationships one day panicked me

And that was when the decision was made. It's time to file for divorce.

Breaking Free

I wish I could say the decision was the hardest part, but it wasn't. What came next tested me in ways I couldn't have imagined.

The hardest part wasn't just making the decision—it was following through.

There were moments when I felt like giving in. When the guilt and fear felt overwhelming, and I wanted to go back to what was familiar, even if it was painful.

But every time I thought about the long-term impact on my daughters, I found the courage to stay the course. They deserved better. And eventually I believed I did, too.

Following through on my decision to actually get divorced wasn't easy. It was scary. Not knowing what the outcome would be. I agonized over it for months, feeling the weight of guilt, doubt, and fear.

What if I was wrong? What if I really was being selfish? What if I am making a mistake?

This is especially true when you are dealing with someone who is an expert at making you feel like you are out of your mind and selfish for doing anything other than what he wanted.

But when I thought about my girls and what kind of role model I wanted to be, I remembered that the selfish thing would be to do nothing. And that gave me the strength I needed to stay the course.

I had to show them that they could stand up for themselves, set boundaries, and that love and respect are non-negotiable.

Every step forward felt like climbing a mountain, but each climb brought me closer to freedom. I chose to settle out of court and save years of more manipulation by "buying my freedom," giving him nearly everything he asked for. All of which were material things.

I trusted that I could rebuild my life on my own—and I did.

Thriving on the Other Side

For the first time in years, I could breathe. And though the journey was far from over, I knew I was on my way to building a life I loved waking up to.

The victory of staying the course and actually finalizing the divorce gave me a new pride in myself and proof that I could do whatever I set my mind to. I just had to believe in myself. And I wasn't going to settle for less again.

My whole life my identity had been tied to meeting others' expectations—being a good daughter, wife, mother, employee—and meeting everyone else's needs but my own.

After the divorce, I began a journey of discovering who I really am—something I couldn't do when I was constantly walking on eggshells or seeking someone else's approval.

I no longer had to do things I didn't want to do just because someone else expected me to. I could choose how I spent my days, and though it was scary at times, it has been incredibly life-alteringly rewarding.

I learned to set boundaries—not just with my former husband, but with everyone in my life. I began to notice patterns of manipulation in friendships and other relationships that I had been blind to before. And I learned to stop apologizing for simply being me.

For the first time, I was free to make my own choices. I didn't need permission anymore to be myself.

Lessons Learned: Insights for You

1. You can't see the label from inside the jar.

I didn't know I was in a cycle of accepting narcissistic behavior because it was all I'd ever known. I didn't realize that what I was enduring wasn't normal. But once I started to see it—really see it—I couldn't unsee it. And that awareness gave me the power to make different choices.

When you're in the thick of manipulation, it's almost impossible to recognize it yourself. That's why it's so important to get support—from therapists, coaches, or friends who truly understand what healthy relationships look like. They can help you see what you can't see and guide you toward a life of freedom and authenticity.

2. You have to be yourself to have true love with anyone else

Before you can truly thrive in any relationship—romantic or otherwise—you have to find and love yourself.

For so long, I thought that sacrificing myself was the price I had to pay to be a good wife, a good mother, and a good person. But I've learned that being true to yourself is not only okay—it's essential.

You can't give your best to others if you're not giving yourself the freedom to be who you are. If you feel like you've lost yourself, know that it's never too late to rediscover who you are.

Surround yourself with people who support you, and release those who don't, seek help if you need it, and trust that you have the strength to break free from whatever is holding you back. Because you do!

3. The best gift you can give to those you love is your authentic self.

For me, that meant showing my daughters what it looks like to live authentically. It meant breaking generational patterns and teaching them, through my actions, that they don't have to settle for anything less than a life they love waking up to.

Today, my daughters are thriving, each in their own beautiful ways.

My youngest, now 15, was able to grow up surrounded by a healthier, freer version of me and of love. She hasn't had to unlearn the same toxic patterns because she's seen a different model of what's possible. She knows what it looks like to live authentically. She shines as her true self—surrounded by friends and family who love her for exactly who she is.

My oldest goes after what she wants with confidence, self-assured, and has mastered the art of setting boundaries. The one who I once worried would grow up to be like me, told me recently, *"I want to be like you someday."* (I know, it made my heart melt, too!)

What I once feared I now could be proud of! Not the woman I *used* to be—trapped, manipulated, and silenced. She was saying she wanted to be like the woman I had *become*: someone who stood up for herself, broke free from toxic patterns, and created a life she loved.

All the tears, all the struggles, the pain endured. The questioning of whether what I was doing was the right thing … all became crystal clear in that moment that every single pain and lesson I had to learn was worth every bit of it.

4. It IS possible to live a life you love waking up to

Today, I am proud to say that I genuinely live a life I love waking up to.

I now live in a beautiful place surrounded by palm trees and ocean views. My daughters are thriving in incredible schools, and I've created a business I love, helping others find the freedom and joy I've discovered.

I went from waking up with dread to looking forward to my days. From a career filled with toxic people to running my own business, helping others create lives they love waking up to.

Life doesn't have to be a drag! And if it feels like it is, it's time to do something about it. You have more control than you may realize! I know this from my own experience and from the experiences of my clients. And it all starts with being who you are here to be and not taking anyone else's shit who tells you otherwise. Pay attention to the choices that make you feel alive, and question the ones that don't.

Even when you can't see a light at the end of the tunnel, I assure you there is a way out of anything that is holding you back.

Helping Others Find Their Path

Today, I help others break free from what holds them back because I know how powerful it is to live a life that truly aligns with your soul.

You deserve more than just going through the motions.

And here's the truth: it's not just possible—it's within your reach.

For resources you can use to build your path to your authentic life that you love waking up to every day, check the link in my bio on the next page!

Stacy McAlpine

Stacy McAlpine, the Founder and CEO of Journey Fuel, is a Life Transformation Specialist dedicated to helping people live lives they love waking up to.

With more than two decades of experience as a Strategic Advisor, Project Manager, and Change Management Consultant with top-tier consulting firms, including PricewaterhouseCoopers and Ernst and Young, Stacy was called in to help some of the largest organizations on the planet (Google, State of California, US Departments of State, Homeland Security and Defense, to name a few) to turn their aspirations into reality. Along the way, Stacy's personal quest for fulfillment led her to innovate the tools and techniques she used with her corporate clients into a reliable system that empowers individuals to achieve their own life change!

Recognizing the profound impact her formula could have on millions of individuals worldwide, Stacy founded Journey Fuel to share this integrated approach to getting results that blends proven strategic planning and change practices with self-development principles, infused with a journey theme to add excitement and playfulness to the process.

With each life transformed, Stacy creates a ripple effect of positive change that extends far beyond individual journeys. As a trusted guide, she is dedicated to supporting and empowering you every step of the way!

Learn more at www.journeyfuel.com

CHAPTER 19

Rewriting the Rules: A Story of Leaving, Healing, and Sexual Freedom

Dr. Toni Bear

Dedicated to every woman who has ever felt unseen, unheard, or unsure of her worth. May this story remind you of your strength, your resilience, and your right to reclaim your voice, your desires, and your life. You are enough, and your journey is just beginning.

I was 24 years old when I walked down the aisle. My heart was full, my smile bright, and my belief in forever unshakable. I was marrying my best friend, the man I thought I would share everything with—

my hopes, my fears, and all those late-night dreams about the future. I didn't just love him; I admired him. Seven years older than me, he seemed so… grown up.

He was everything I thought I wasn't yet. He had stories of past relationships, years in the workforce, and a confidence I wanted to wrap myself in. I, on the other hand, was still figuring myself out. Sure, I was an adult on paper—teaching full time, earning my master's degree, and coaching three sports—but inside? I was still emotionally and sexually inexperienced. To be honest, I was more like a teenager playing dress-up, hoping no one would notice how much I didn't know.

The first few months of marriage were filled with optimism. Love was supposed to be enough, right? We laughed at the same jokes, played tennis and basketball together, and had big plans for the future. But as the newness wore off, a quiet unease crept in—something I didn't yet know how to name.

He had expectations—especially when it came to our sex life. We'd been sexual for four years before marriage, but now he wanted excitement, the kind he'd seen in porn or experienced with previous girlfriends. And I… I was just trying to figure out how to be comfortable in my own skin. His words stung: "Why don't you enjoy this more? What's wrong with you?"

What was wrong with me? That question haunted me. I wanted to be the wife he dreamed of, but the truth was, I was still carrying wounds I hadn't unpacked yet. My childhood had been steeped in shadows I rarely talked about, and those shadows left me unsure, shy, and clueless about how to explore intimacy the way he wanted.

At the same time, I was growing in other areas. Teaching full time, studying for my master's, and coaching gave me confidence and independence. But the more I grew, the more our relationship felt less like a partnership and more like a tug-of-war. The love was still there, but so was the growing distance. He wanted something I wasn't, and I grew unhappier by the day.

The Cracks Begin to Show

The first time I realized something was seriously wrong, we were sitting on the couch watching TV. During a commercial, he commented, "You know, it's like you don't even enjoy sex. It's not normal."

I froze. My stomach knotted. My face burned. I wanted to argue, to tell him he was wrong, but deep down, I wasn't so sure he was. Something *did* feel off, didn't it? I was trying—God, I was trying so hard. But sex felt less like something we shared and more like another test I was failing. After all, he had already cut me off sexually and told me I wanted it too often, suggesting I should masturbate more.

In the days that followed, I played that comment in my head, over and over. *What's wrong with you? Why can't you just be normal?* His words didn't even make sense—one minute, I wanted sex too much; the next, I didn't want it enough. It was a cycle I couldn't win.

Whenever I tried to talk to him about it, to figure out where we'd gone wrong, he ignored me. Eventually, he stopped talking to me altogether. I stopped bringing it up—what was the point? Every attempt to connect felt like hitting a wall. He had decided there was something wrong with me, and no amount of effort seemed to change his mind.

Inside, the doubts festered. I started questioning everything about myself—not just in the bedroom, but everywhere. Was I not fun enough? Too ambitious? Too serious? My days were packed with lesson plans, study sessions, and coaching. I was growing into a version of myself I'd never imagined, but instead of pride, all I felt was guilt. Guilt for not being what he wanted. Guilt for not knowing how to fix us.

I sought therapy, hoping to make sense of my feelings. I poured myself into work. But no matter how much I achieved, I couldn't silence the voice in my head whispering, *"You're failing."*

Then came the night I sat in my car outside our house, gripping the steering wheel, unable to go inside. It had been weeks of the silent treatment, and I knew that if I walked through that door, I'd feel smaller, quieter, less myself. The cracks in our relationship, once invisible, were now everywhere. And for the first time, I started to wonder: *Was this what marriage was supposed to feel like?*

The Turning Point: Deciding to Leave

The night I knew I had to leave wasn't dramatic. There were no shouting matches or slammed doors. It was quiet—so quiet I could hear the clock ticking in the living room. I sat on the couch, staring at the TV, while he worked upstairs. Inside, I was replaying the same thoughts I'd been carrying for weeks: *Is this it?*

Earlier that day, he'd snapped at me because I called him at work. Something shifted. For the first time, I wondered: *What if he's not right? What if the problem isn't me?*

The hardest part wasn't admitting I needed to leave. It was imagining what would come next—telling family and friends, dividing our lives, starting over. And then there was the guilt. My husband wasn't a bad person. He loved me the best way he knew how. But his love came with conditions, and I couldn't meet them.

When I finally said the words, "I can't do this anymore," he looked at me like I'd spoken a foreign language. For the first time in years, I didn't doubt myself. Leaving wasn't easy, but staying was slowly breaking me. I needed to leave, to breathe, to heal.

The Aftermath: Finding Myself Again

The first morning after I moved out, I woke up in the bed of my childhood in my parents' house. The sheets smelled like home and comfort, but my chest felt tight, like I'd forgotten how to breathe. I lay there, staring at the ceiling, trying to make sense of what I'd just done.

The silence was deafening. For years, my life had been filled with the hum of routines, making dinner, and the constant background noise of someone else's presence. Now, it was just me, mom, and dad. No one asked why I wasn't happy. They loved me without condition. Just me, alone and lost in my thoughts ....

I sat with myself in silence and started to cry. It wasn't the delicate kind of crying you see in movies—it was ugly, heaving sobs that left me gasping for air. And when the tears finally stopped, I felt something I hadn't felt in years: relief.

That was the turning point. Slowly, I began to piece myself back together. I continued with therapy—a decision that terrified me at first. I sat across from a stranger unpacking years of shame and doubt. Therapy felt like ripping off a BAND-AID that had been holding me together. But as hard as it was, it was also liberating. For the first time, I had a space to tell the whole truth about my marriage, my fears, and the wounds I'd carried since childhood. And in that space, I started to see myself more clearly. I started asking, *What do I want?*

The answer wasn't always clear, but for the first time in years, I felt like I was heading in the right direction. I wasn't just surviving anymore—I was starting to live. And the more I leaned into that, the more I realized: losing my marriage wasn't the end of my story. It was the beginning of a new chapter.

Reclaiming My Sexual Self

The first time I stood in front of the mirror, really looking at myself, it was uncomfortable. I'd spent years avoiding that kind of honesty. I knew how to glance, but this was different. This was about seeing all of me—the woman I was, not the one I thought I was supposed to be.

At first, all I could see were the flaws: the weight I gained during the marriage, the places where gravity had taken its toll, the scars no one else noticed but me. But then I caught my own eye, and something shifted. I thought about how much this body had carried me through … heartbreak, late nights, early mornings, the weight of expectations. And I thought, *If I can handle all of that, why can't I handle loving myself?*

That was the day I decided to stop apologizing for who I was, especially in the bedroom. For so long, I'd been convinced I wasn't enough—too shy, too inexperienced, too damaged. My ex had made it seem like sex was something I failed at, but the truth was, I'd never really given myself the chance to figure out what *I wanted.*

So, I made a promise to myself: I would find out.

It started with books. I bought ones about sexuality, intimacy, and pleasure—ones I'd been too embarrassed to even pick up before. I wasn't just learning about sex; I was learning about *me.* Then I took it a step further. I started dating and having casual sex. A lover asked a simple question: *"When was the last time you felt truly connected to your body?"*

I couldn't answer. I didn't even know what that meant. But by the end of that two-year relationship, I'd started to understand. Through touch, sensual sexual contact, and open conversations, I began to see my body not as something that needed to be fixed, but as something that deserved to be celebrated. It was awkward at first—like learning a new language—but it was also thrilling.

I gave myself permission to explore. I tried things I'd never dared to before, both alone and with new partners. I asked questions, spoke up about what I liked and didn't like, and let myself be curious. For the first time, sex wasn't about performance or pleasing someone else. It was about *me*—what felt good, what made me laugh, what lit me up.

Reclaiming my sexual self wasn't just about sex—it was about power. It was about taking back the parts of me I'd been taught to be ashamed of and learning to love them fiercely. And once I did, I couldn't help but wonder what else I'd been holding back.

Because if I could claim this part of my life, there was nothing else I couldn't take on.

Building a Life on My Own Terms

The first time I laughed—*really* laughed—after the divorce, it surprised me. I was sitting at a coffee shop with a friend, sipping an over-priced latte and venting about the ridiculous things I'd done in the past month … like trying to assemble IKEA furniture by myself. At some point, we were both doubled over, tears streaming down our faces. It wasn't just funny; it was freeing.

For the first time in years, I wasn't walking on eggshells. I wasn't worried about saying the wrong thing or being judged. I was just … me. And I liked her. My life was a blank canvas, and for the first time, I was the only one holding the brush. It was exhilarating—and terrifying.

Work became a place where I thrived. I poured my energy into my teaching, my coaching, and eventually my dreams beyond the class-room. I moved from the east to the west coast, and enrolled in a doctoral program. With every new project, every new challenge, I felt myself growing stronger. I wasn't just surviving anymore—I was soaring.

But it wasn't all smooth sailing. There were nights when the loneliness crept in, whispering that I'd made a mistake. Friends were helpful, but they couldn't fill the silence of an empty apartment or the ache of missing what I'd thought was my forever. It was during those nights that I learned the value of sitting with discomfort, of letting it pass without trying to fix it. I'd pour a cup of tea, grab my journal, and remind myself: *This is temporary. I'm building something better.*

What I've learned is this: Building a life on your own terms isn't about perfection or having it all figured out. It's about showing up every day and choosing yourself. It's about finding beauty in chaos, strength in the struggle, and joy in the simplest things.

It's about realizing that the life you're creating, with all its ups and downs, is the one you were always meant to live. And that's worth everything.

The Journey to Empower Others

The first time someone asked me for advice about their marriage, I didn't know whether to laugh or cry. We were sitting in a café. She glanced at me and said, "You seem so … sure of yourself now. How did you do it?"

Sure, of myself? Me? If only she knew how many nights I'd spent crying into a pint of ice cream, questioning every decision I'd ever made. But as I listened to her talk about her struggles—the constant criticism, the loneliness that came from being in a relationship that didn't feel like a partnership—I realized something. She wasn't looking for someone perfect. She was looking for someone who had been there, who understood.

So, I told her my story. Not the polished version, but the messy, raw truth about how I'd had to rebuild my life from the ground up. How I'd learned to stop listening to everyone else's expectations and start trusting my own instincts. How I'd finally started to believe that I deserved more than just "good enough."

That moment stuck with me. I realized that the lessons I'd learned—the hard, uncomfortable, life-changing lessons—weren't just for me. They were for every woman who had ever felt like she wasn't enough. For every woman who had been told she needed to fit into someone else's mold, who had been made to feel small, who had forgotten how powerful she really was.

I started small, just like I had on my own journey. I shared my sexual reawakening story with friends, then with friends of friends, and eventually with complete strangers. I joined groups, led workshops, wrote articles, and spoke from stages about everything I'd learned—about love, healing, and reclaiming your life after it falls apart. I wanted women to see what I had finally seen in myself—that they weren't broken, that they didn't need to be "fixed," that they were already enough.

That's why I share this story with you. That's why I've turned my pain into my mission to help others. Because every time I see a woman step into her power, every time I hear her say, "I'm ready to choose myself," it reminds me of the woman I used to be—the one who sat in her car, gripping the steering wheel, wondering if she'd ever be brave enough to leave.

And now? Now, I get to watch other women find that same bravery. I get to see them reclaim their lives, their dreams, and their sense of self.

And there's nothing more empowering than that.

Closing Reflections: A Life of My Own

The first time I felt truly free, I was standing on a cliff overlooking the ocean on Thanksgiving Day. It was one of those postcard-perfect days, with the waves crashing below and the sun painting the sky in shades of gold and pink. I'd given up all my material possessions, moved to California for graduate school, and was uncertain about the future. There was no plan, no schedule, no one waiting for me to explain where I was or what I was doing. It was just me, the sea and the wind whipping through my hair.

This was my life in my 30s. Messy, imperfect, but *mine*.

Getting there wasn't easy. There were moments I wanted to give up, when the fear of starting over felt like too much to bear. But every time I doubt myself, I think about the woman I want to become—the one who won't settle, who doesn't shrink, who doesn't let fear dictate her choices. And little by little, I built a life that felt like it belonged to her.

Looking back, I don't regret the marriage. I don't regret the pain, the struggle, or even the mistakes I made along the way. Because every one of those moments led me here. They taught me resilience, self-worth, and the power of choosing myself—even when it was the hardest thing I'd ever done.

I've learned that it's okay that my life isn't perfect or fit in with someone else's five-year plan. It can be wild and unpredictable, full of detours, and second chances. It can be whatever you make it, as long as it's true to you.

So, here's what I want you to know, whoever you are, wherever you are on your journey: It's never too late to start over. It's never too late to choose yourself, to rewrite the story you've been told about who you are and what you deserve.

Because the truth is, you are enough. You always have been. And once you realize that, once you stop waiting for someone else to give you permission to live the life you want, everything changes.

Standing on that cliff, with the sun setting and the wind carrying my past out to sea, I made a promise to myself: I will never settle for less than I deserve again.

And that's a promise I intend to keep.

Dr. Toni Bear

Dr. Toni Bear is a renowned sexologist, educator, and author dedicated to empowering women to embrace their authentic selves and rewrite their life stories after divorce. With over two decades of experience in teaching, coaching, and mentoring, she blends academic expertise with personal resilience to guide women through profound transformations.

Marrying her best friend at 24, Dr. Toni faced a marriage that, despite its joys, left her feeling unseen and uncertain about her desires and identity. Her eventual divorce became the turning point for a journey of healing, self-discovery, and empowerment. Therapy and introspection allowed her to reclaim her voice and redefine her relationships with intimacy and love.

Dr. Toni's experiences fueled her pursuit of a doctorate specializing in sexuality, inspiring her career dedicated to helping women rediscover their power and pleasure. She combines evidence-based practices with heartfelt empathy, offering workshops and programs on sexual empowerment, navigating life transitions, and building authentic lives. Her clients describe her as a compassionate guide who sparks courage and transformation.

Believing life after divorce is a new beginning, Dr. Toni empowers women to rewrite their narratives and fully embrace life. Based in Pennsylvania, she enjoys hiking, writing, and engaging with her vibrant community of friends, family, and clients.

Connect with Dr. Toni at https://www.tonibearedd.com.

Afterword

Your Chapter Awaits

Dear Reader,

As you turn this final page, you might find yourself reflecting on the journey you've just experienced through these words. Each story you read is a tapestry of dreams, struggles, triumphs, and the relentless spirit of its creator. Now, imagine a world where your story joins these ranks – where your voice, your experiences, and your unique perspective are shared and celebrated.

This is not just an invitation; it's a call to action from <u>Action Takers Publishing</u>. We believe in the power of stories to transform, inspire, and connect humankind. More importantly, we believe in your story and its potential to make a significant impact on the planet.

Why wait for "someday" to tell your story? The time is now, and the world is ready to listen. Whether it's a tale of adventure, a deeply personal memoir, a groundbreaking idea, or a story that has been quietly growing in your heart, it deserves to be told.

At Action Takers Publishing, led by our Founder & CEO, Lynda Sunshine West, we specialize in turning visions into reality. We understand the journey of transforming a personal narrative into a published book – it's a journey of courage, creativity, and breaking through fears. Our team is dedicated to guiding you through every step of this exhilarating process, from the initial draft to the moment your book is held in the hands of eager readers across the globe.

Join our vibrant community of authors, a diverse group of storytellers who have dared to make their voices heard. With us, you'll find more than just a publisher; you'll discover a supportive network of mentors, editors, and fellow authors who are all committed to the success of your story.

Take the leap. Embrace the thrill of seeing your name on the cover of your very own book. Contact us at Action Takers Publishing, and let's embark on this remarkable journey together. Your story matters, and the time to share it with the world is now.

Nothing Happens Without Action.

Lynda Sunshine West

Founder & CEO

Action Takers Publishing

https://www.actiontakerspublishing.com/

p.s. Remember, every great story begins with a simple decision to start writing. Yours is no different. Let's make it happen, together.